HAZEL OFFNER

WITH DALE & SANDY LARSEN

A Deeper Look at the

FRUIT *of the* SPIRIT

NINE SESSIONS FOR GROUPS AND INDIVIDUALS

GROWING IN THE
LIKENESS OF CHRIST

LifeGuide®
IN DEPTH
BIBLE STUDIES

IVP Connect

An imprint of InterVarsity Press
Downers Grove, Illinois

InterVarsity Press
P.O. Box 1400, Downers Grove, IL 60515-1426
World Wide Web: www.ivpress.com
E-mail: email@ivpress.com

P	24	23	22	21	20	19	18	17	16	15	14	13	12	11	10	9	8	7	6	5	4	3	2	1
Y	34	33	32	31	30	29	28	27	26	25	24	23	22	21	20	19	18	17	16	15	14	13		

CONTENTS

INTRODUCTION

Growing in the Likeness of Christ

God has changed my life through small group Bible studies. In Urbana, where I live, we have several hundred people studying in small groups all over the community each year. As I have worked with the leaders of these small groups, I have watched God use the Bible and group interaction to change their lives too. No other method that I have seen has been so effective in helping people really get to know God.

The original *Fruit of the Spirit* LifeGuide Bible study emerged after our groups had just finished studying several books in both the Old and New Testaments. A friend of mine said, "Why don't you give us a change of pace and write some topical studies on the fruit of the Spirit in Galatians 5:22-23?" I thought about the verses—"But the fruit of the Spirit is love, joy, peace, patience, kindness, goodness, faithfulness, gentleness and self-control. Against such things there is no law." How could a worthwhile study be written about single virtues that were explained by only one word? It is exciting to realize that all these virtues are inside Christians because the Holy Spirit has taken up residence within us. But I wondered if there was some way to show how this fruit could be lived out in practical ways. How, for example, can we actually appropriate the fruit of peace when we are worried? Or how can we experience the fruit of joy if life is tumbling down all around us?

The *Fruit of the Spirit* LifeGuide, which makes up part one of each session in this guide and serves as the springboard for the rest of the sections, was a result of this exploration. I saw the fruit of joy illustrated in the disciples on seeing their risen Lord; the fruit of faithful-

ness sprang alive as Jehoshaphat and the outnumbered army of Israel became aware of God's steady presence; and I recognized God's patience with me in a new way as I contemplated Christ's tender forgiveness of Peter. The writing of the guide truly changed my perspective on people and circumstances in my own life.

When InterVarsity Press approached me about expanding my LifeGuide into the larger LifeGuide in Depth resource you have in your hands, I started to think back on the situations—the places and ways God was ripening the fruit of the Spirit in my life as I was working through each fruit to create the Life-Guide—and thought it might encourage you to hear how I was being changed by my study of each fruit. I've therefore added brief stories from my own life at the end of part one in each session. I hope these "Thoughts from Hazel" sections will inspire you in your walk with the Spirit and help you notice even the seemingly small ways God is at work in you, developing the fruit of his Spirit in deeper ways.

Parts two through four of this new in-depth LifeGuide have been written by Dale and Sandy Larsen, who graciously agreed to dive into their own deep study of these passages and reflect on the Spirit's fruit in their own life. Through their personal stories in the "Reflect" parts and by tracing the nature of God through the grand story of Scripture in the "Connect: Scripture to Scripture" segments, they'll lead you in seeing how God is the source of each fruit and the one who helps us live each one out in our own circumstances.

In the years since I wrote the original *Fruit of the Spirit* guide, the different fruits have become more meaningful as I have experienced life in deeper relationship with the *giver* and *source* of the fruit. This isn't surprising, if you think about it. The apostle Paul's now-famous list of the fruit of the Spirit in chapter 5 of his letter to the Galatians surely came from his own intimate relationship with God; he could name the fruit because he himself had experienced the Spirit and seen the fruit evident in his own life as the Spirit changed his heart. And he knew how powerful living out the Spirit's fruit would be for the Galatians, in the midst of the pagan culture they lived in and the lies and rules being imposed on them by false teachers. The essential message he passed on to them is the truth I discovered as I wrote the *Fruit of the Spirit* LifeGuide: turn to Jesus and learn the way of the Spirit—the way that brings freedom and life to you and to those around you.

God's highest purpose for each person he's made—from Adam and Eve to the Galatians to us today—hasn't changed: He wants to make us like Jesus (Romans 8:29). As we fulfill this purpose by getting to know our Lord better and by obeying him, we will exhibit the fruit of the Spirit whether we are aware of it or not. In these days when our world is so fragmented and confused and when sin is so flagrant, just one person who exhibits this fruit of God's Spirit can make a difference. Nothing attracts unbelievers and believers alike to God as much as seeing a life lived out in love, joy, peace, gentleness and so forth, even though that person may be suffering. A life exhibiting these beautiful qualities can be a powerful tool of evangelism as well as for promoting harmony and unity in the body of Christ.

Our hope for you in this new resource, then, is the same as Paul's desire for the Galatians: that understanding and experiencing the love, joy, peace, patience, kindness, goodness, faithfulness, gentleness and self-control of God will lead you to a deeper love for him and to a life that more fully reflects him. May we all more

and more relinquish ourselves to the One who has implanted his Spirit within us.

HOW TO USE LIFEGUIDE® IN DEPTH

The Bible is God's Word to his people. In it and through it we find life and wisdom for life. Most importantly, the Scriptures point us to Christ, who is the culmination of God's revelation to us of who he is. The LifeGuide in Depth Bible Study series has been created for those who want to go deeply into the Bible and deeply into Christ.

Going deeply will require time and effort. But the reward will be well worth it. If your desire is a richer understanding of God's Word, if you want to grasp Scripture at a level and in dimensions you've not engaged in before, these in-depth studies are for you.

This series emphasizes

- taking passages seriously as a whole

- seeing how each passage connects to and is built on the rest of Scripture

- applying the truth of each passage to individuals and to our Christian communities

How do we do this? Each session follows a four-part format:

- **Part 1. Investigate**—Getting an overview of the passage as a whole.

- **Part 2. Connect: Scripture to Scripture**—Seeing how the passage or theme connects to other parts of the Bible.

- **Part 3. Reflect**—Pondering a key theme in the passage through a short reading.

- **Part 4. Discuss: Putting It All Together**—Tying together as a group the various themes from the first three parts and learning to apply the passage to real life.

Though groups and individuals may use LifeGuide in Depth studies in different ways and formats, the most straightforward way to use the guides is for individuals to study the first three sections on their own before each group meeting. Those first three sections are best done over several days rather than in one sitting, as individuals will typically need a total of three to four hours to work through them. Part four then offers a forty-five to sixty-minute group discussion that guides members in putting together everything they've learned.

LifeGuide in Depth Bible Studies can be used by people of various ages, from teenagers to seniors and everyone in between. Groups can be church-related home small groups and Sunday-school classes, women's and men's Bible studies, neighborhood Bible studies, and university campus small groups. And the guides can be used on a weekly or biweekly basis, or could even form the core of a retreat weekend.

AN OVERVIEW OF THE FOUR PARTS

Part 1. Investigate (On Your Own). Inductive Bible study is at the core of LifeGuide in Depth studies. Allowing for in-depth study of one passage, an inductive approach to Scripture has three main parts: we first carefully observe what is in the text, then interpret what we are to learn from what we observe and finally apply the meaning of the passage to our own lives. This is accomplished through the use of open-ended questions that help people discover the Bible for themselves. The goal is to come to the passage with fresh eyes, not supposing we know all that it means ahead of time, but looking to see what God might have to teach us anew.

Inductive study is not meant to be mechanical; Scripture is not data that we manipulate toward a certain output. Nor does it imply that we can master Scripture. Rather we expect the Word to master us. But believing that God uses our understanding to touch our hearts and that he uses our hearts to touch our understanding, inductive study can help us draw near to God. It's a tool to guide our hearts and minds toward Christ through his Word. For more on inductive study we recommend *Transforming Bible*

Study by Bob Grahmann and *The Bible Study Handbook* by Lindsay Olesberg.

Part one of each session is a revised edition of the original LifeGuide Bible study guide. LifeGuide Bible studies have been the leading series for individuals and groups studying Scripture for almost thirty years. They have given millions of people a solid grasp of the Bible. The LifeGuide in Depth Bible Study series, like the original LifeGuides, honors the context of each book of the Bible and the original message of each biblical author, and guides readers into application of God's Word. Relevant excerpts from *The IVP Bible Background Commentary: New Testament* and *The IVP Bible Background Commentary: Old Testament* have been added to these studies to offer helpful historical and cultural information about each passage. These excerpts appear as callouts in part one of each guide.

Part 2. Connect: Scripture to Scripture (On Your Own). One of the most important ways of understanding any particular passage of Scripture is to uncover how it stands in the pathway of the rest of Scripture. The historical, cultural and literary background of any passage is critical, and how biblical writers draw on previous Scripture offers a wealth of meaning to readers. The purpose of part two of each session is to draw this out.

The original writers and readers of the books of the Bible were thoroughly immersed in the Scripture written beforehand. It was the air they breathed. So when they wrote, earlier Scripture passages and themes were an inseparable part of how they thought and taught. Thus, understanding the New Testament often requires knowing the Old Testament allusions, themes or direct quotations found there. And usually it is not enough to know the one particular Old Testament verse being quoted or referenced. We need to understand the context of that verse in the chapter and book in which it is found. Neglecting this can lead readers astray in their interpretations or applications.

For example, in Mark 6:47-50, Jesus walks on the lake during a storm and is "about to pass by [the disciples]" (v. 48), who are struggling for survival in a boat. Does Jesus not see them? Doesn't he care they are in danger? Why does he intend to "pass by"? What's going on? The answer is found by going back to the Old Testament. In Exodus 33:19–34:7 and 1 Kings 19:10-11, God "passes by" Moses and Elijah to reveal himself in a clear and dramatic way. Mark uses the same phrase (which his readers would recognize) to indicate that Jesus is making a similar dramatic revelation of divine character.

In making these connections, it is usually more helpful to go backward than to go forward. That is, we should first investigate Scripture written before the passage being studied was written. For instance, in seeking to understand the Psalms, we should first go to the earlier books of the Old Testament rather than to the New Testament. The psalmists knew and perhaps had memorized large portions of Genesis, Exodus and so forth. That was the raw material they were working with; those were their sources. If we don't understand how and why they built on these, we won't understand fully what they are saying.

Take the "suffering servant" of Isaiah 52–53. Although New Testament writers linked Jesus to the suffering servant, we shouldn't "read back" into Isaiah the notion that the servant was a divine figure. The text in Isaiah does not indicate that and we would be misreading the text to insist that it does. Nonetheless, it is entirely appropriate to use this image, as Jesus did, to gain a greater understanding of another dimension of who Jesus was and what he came to do.

In part two, then, we will mostly, but not exclusively, go back to Scripture that predates the passage we are studying for better understanding.

Part 3. Reflect (On Your Own). In part three you will find a reading that expands on one of the themes of the study. It may contain a story or commentary on the passage, or both. And it may be drawn from some other Christian author or source, whether contemporary or ancient. In any case, it is intended to help focus your mind in a single direction after the wide variety of issues raised in parts one and two. A couple of questions at the end of the reading will help you crystallize what you have learned.

Part 4. Discuss: Putting It All Together (With a Group). This part is, as the name describes, intended for group discussion. You can work through it on your own too, but some questions are repetitive with questions from the first three parts. This is intentional and necessary for group discussion; after individuals in a group have worked through each passage on their own during the week, they will want to hear from each other what they have learned and thought about. If you decide you do want to go through part four by yourself anyway, you can skip those questions that were found earlier or use those questions as opportunities to think again about key ideas. Reviewing the content is a good way for groups *and* individuals to lock those ideas into their hearts and minds.

Groups should begin the discussion with the "Open" question and then read the passage together. Everyone will have been over the passage several times already, but reading aloud in a group can actually bring new insight.

Below are a few suggestions for group members that can facilitate rich discussion and insight:

1. Come to the study prepared. Follow the suggestions for individual study mentioned above. You will find that careful preparation will greatly enrich your time spent in group discussion.

2. Be willing to participate in the discussion. The leader of your group will not be lecturing. Instead, she or he will be asking the questions found in this guide and encouraging the members of the group to

discuss what they have learned.

3. Stick to the topic being discussed. These studies focus on a particular passage of Scripture. This allows everyone to participate on equal ground and fosters in-depth study.

4. Be sensitive to the other members of the group. Listen attentively when they describe what they have learned. You may be surprised by their insights! Also note that each question assumes a variety of answers; many questions do not have "right" answers, particularly questions that aim at meaning or application. Instead the questions push us to explore the passage more thoroughly.

    When possible, link what you say to the comments of others. Also, be affirming whenever you can. This will encourage some of the more hesitant members of the group to participate.

5. Be careful not to dominate the discussion. We are sometimes so eager to express our thoughts that we leave too little opportunity for others to respond. By all means participate! But allow others to do so also.

6. Expect God to teach you through the passage being discussed and through the other members of the group. Pray that you will have an enjoyable and profitable time together, but also that as a result of the study you will find ways to take action individually and/or as a group.

7. It will be helpful for groups to follow a few basic guidelines. These guidelines, which you may wish to adapt to your situation, should be read at the beginning of the first session.

    - Anything said in the group is considered confidential and will not be discussed outside the group unless specific permission is given to do so.
    - We will provide time for each person present to talk if he or she feels comfortable doing so.
    - We will talk about ourselves and our own situations, avoiding conversation about other people.
    - We will listen attentively to each other.
    - We will be very cautious about giving advice.

    Additional suggestions for the group leader can be found at the back of the guide.

Plunging into the depths of God's wisdom and love is a glorious adventure. Like Paul said in 1 Corinthians 2:9-10: "As it is written: 'What no eye has seen, what no ear has heard, and what no human mind has conceived'—the things God has prepared for those who love him—these are the things God has revealed to us by his Spirit. The Spirit searches all things, even the deep things of God." As you go in depth into Scripture, may the Spirit reveal the deep things of God's own self to you.

LOVE

1 John 4:7-16

WHERE WE'RE GOING[*]

Part 1. Investigate: 1 John 4:7-16 (On Your Own)

Part 2. Connect: Scripture to Scripture (On Your Own)

Part 3. Reflect: Love's Evidence (On Your Own)

Part 4. Discuss: Putting It All Together (With a Group)

A PRAYER TO PRAY

Here's a prayer to get you started:

God of love, you show us that love is not just an abstract idea. Love is a Person. You have lived among us and offered us your love, love which we could never deserve. You fill us with your Spirit of love and help us extend your love to others. Without you, our so-called love is cold and selfish. We know what love is only because Christ gave his life for us. Purify us with the fire of your sacrificial love. Show us where our love is lacking; change our hearts and move us forward to put love into action. Amen.

---

[*]Though these studies can be used in a variety of ways and formats, for maximum benefit we recommend doing parts one, two and three on your own and then working through the questions in part four with a group.

PART 1. INVESTIGATE
1 John 4:7-16
(On Your Own)

Introduction to 1 John: *If the setting of 1 John is the same as that of the Fourth Gospel, it is meant to encourage Christians expelled from the synagogues, some of whose colleagues have returned to the synagogue by denying Jesus' messiahship (2:19, 22; 4:2-3). . . . But John was concerned about situations in cities other than those addressed in his Gospel. Christians were . . . [being] tempted with the heresy of compromise elsewhere, including compromise with idolatry advocated by false prophets (Rev 2:14-15, 20-23; cf. 1 Jn 4:1; 5:21).*

Read 1 John 4:7-16.

1. According to verses 7-8, where does love come from?

2. Verses 9-10 say that Christ's incarnation and death show us God's love. How do these two events help you to understand God's love?

3. How does God's love motivate you to love others (vv. 11-12)?

4. What basis do we have for the assurance of love (vv. 13-16)?

5. Based on your responses to questions one through four, write a one-sentence description of love.

4:12. *The false teachers may have been claiming to have had mystical visions of God, but John includes a corrective: God was unseen (Ex 33:20), and the sense in which believers could envision him is in his character of love fleshed out in the cross (4:9) and in Christians' sacrificial love (4:12).*

What significance does this kind of love have for you?

6. How have you seen God's love demonstrated through other Christians?

7. Because God is love, what do we know about those whose lives are full of love (v. 16)? Explain.

8. No one has ever seen wind, energy or electrons. We see only the effects of what they do. Likewise, no one has ever seen the love of God. As you look again at this whole passage, in what ways can you see the effects of God's love?

4:13-16. *Although the Qumran community [those who wrote the Dead Sea Scrolls] as a group claimed to possess the Spirit, most of ancient Judaism relegated the Spirit's most dramatic works to the distant past and future, or to very rare individuals. For John, all true believers in Jesus have the Spirit, who moves them to love and prophetically endows them to testify the truth about Christ.*

9. Think of someone you find it especially hard to feel warm toward, someone you are thrown together with regularly. Why is it difficult for you to love that person?

10. Recognizing that love is not based on feelings, what are some practical ways you can show the fruit of love to that person?

Choose a specific action you will take in this coming week to show the fruit of love to this person. Pray specifically about the steps you will take toward loving this person, asking God to manifest this fruit in your life.

THOUGHTS FROM HAZEL

When I was writing these studies back in 1976, there was a woman (now long gone) in our church whom I avoided if at all possible. It seemed as though she was always showing up in my life, however. At church suppers, she'd be seated across the table from me. After church she'd be the first one I ran into in the foyer. And one time at a wedding reception, she and her husband (who was just as bad as she was) were seated at the same table as Dave and me—a table that seated only six people. The other two people at our table were a mother who seemed to be the silent type and her teenage daughter who had brought homework to do. The reception went on for three hours!

The problem? This woman and her husband talked about themselves *all the time:* the trips they'd taken (every little detail with a few pictures stored in their wallets), the sicknesses they and their parents had endured or were presently enduring, their longtime ministry to orphans (a three-hour lecture!). We tried to break in at points. But breaking in often involved asking a question, which led to more and more details of the current subject. For instance, I began talking about the latest book I was reading, and wouldn't you know it—she was reading it too, and she had definite ideas about how the author *should* have told the story. At the end of that evening, I had had it. I resolved never to be caught in that woman's presence again, and for about a year, I never was. But my deep resentment went on. Every time I'd see her, I seethed.

Then came this study on love, particularly questions nine and ten. Guess who popped right into my mind after I had oh-so-spiritually written those two questions? Yep, you got it—this woman who drove me crazy! The Lord nudged me to practically show the fruit of love to her. So I thought. I prayed. And the Holy Spirit *lovingly* gave me the idea of simply walking across the church that next Sunday and saying hello to her.

So that's what I did. That's *all* I did. She was whisked away somehow, and I don't recall ever really talking to her again before they left the church. But my heart sang! Such a little thing, but in God's sight such a huge thing in that I had obeyed the Spirit's prompting. *This* is that thing called love.

PART 2. CONNECT
Scripture to Scripture
(On Your Own)

JOHN'S AUTHORITY TO SPEAK ABOUT GOD'S LOVE

We once heard a Christian say, "God in the New Testament is loving, but God in the Old Testament was terrible." Many people have the same idea. They believe that a God of love is a radical New Testament innovation, introduced by Jesus Christ.

If God was once terrible and is now loving, then somewhere between the Old and New Testaments, his character must have changed. Intellectually we know that can't be true. God does not change. Still, whether it makes sense or not, many people believe that the God of the Old Testament is a different sort of God from the God in the New Testament: a God who exhibits wrath rather than love.

If anyone could write with authority about love—both the love of God and our love for one another—it was John the apostle, the author of this letter. Tradition has it that he was "the disciple whom Jesus loved" (Jn 13:23) and was one of the three disciples closest to Jesus. John holds that love is so inseparable from the character of God that "everyone who loves has been born of God and knows God. Whoever does not love does not know God, because God is love" (vv. 7-8).

God is love. There could be no stronger declaration that God is a loving God. But has God always been the God of love? Let's look backward into the Old Testament and examine the evidence there for John's declaration.

THE LORD MAKES PROMISES

Abraham (then called Abram) came from a family who worshiped various gods (Joshua 24:2). They migrated northwest from modern-day Iraq to the edge of what is now Turkey. There, apparently out of the blue, the Lord spoke to Abraham and told him to pick up and leave and go to a land which the Lord would show him. Abraham obeyed, and after some sidetracks, he and his immediate family arrived in Canaan. (See Genesis 12–14.)

God had promised Abraham a nation of descendants. The problem was that Abraham and his wife, Sarah, were already old and had no children at all. When the Lord once again spoke reassuring words to Abraham, Abraham expressed severe doubts about the situation.

Read Genesis 15.

In Abraham's circumstances, if you were asked to count the stars and believe that your offspring would be as numerous, what would you think?

_____

_____

_____

_____

_____

Abraham asked how he would know that God's promise was true. In answer, God made a covenant with Abraham (vv. 9-19). How was the covenant evidence that God loved and cared for Abraham?

_____

_____

_____

_____

_____

OUT OF EGYPT

In fulfillment of what God had told Abraham (Genesis 15:13-14), Abraham's great-grandson Joseph was taken to Egypt as a slave. He rose to prominence in the kingdom and was eventually joined there by his father, Jacob, and his brothers. When a new Pharaoh arose, the fortunes of the Israelites changed. They lost all status and became forced laborers for the Egyptians.

After four hundred years of slavery in Egypt, the Israelites were freed under the leadership of Moses and Aaron. They went out into the desert of Sinai with the land of Canaan as their ultimate destination. We don't have to read very far in Deuteronomy before we uncover more about the love of God. At this point in the journey, Moses was looking ahead to the people's entry into Canaan. He wanted to equip them to live there and flourish under the Lord's protection.

Read Deuteronomy 7:7-11. Check the statement(s) that correctly describe why God chose Israel as his people.

____ They were the most numerous people group in the land.
____ God knew that they were the least sinful people on earth at that time.
____ God always keeps his promises, and he had promised to redeem them from Egypt.
____ They had proven their love for and loyalty to God.
____ They were the smallest and least significant nation.
____ He loved them.

God "set his affection" on the nation of Israel. Why? Because he loved them and was keeping his promise. *He loved them because he loved them.* Here is no dispassionate definition of love. It is rather a rationale that defies logic. The origin of God's love is not in the status or goodness of Israel; it is in the character of God. God loved because he loved, with no other explanation.

Read Deuteronomy 6:4-5 and 10:12-15.

Alongside the arrow pointing from God to the people, write what God had done for the Israelites.

God
⇩
the people

_____

_____

_____

_____

Alongside the arrow pointing from the people to God, write what God asked the Israelites to do.

God
⇧
the people

_____

_____

_____

_____

STEADFAST LOVE

Although Israel failed to do what God wanted, in his faithful love he did not abandon his people. The love of God is most commonly expressed in the Old Testament by the Hebrew word *hesed*. Variously translated as "steadfast love," "loving-kindness" or "mercy," *hesed* is not a generalized warm feeling. It assumes a deeply involved personal relationship of loyalty and commitment.

Forty years after the exodus from Egypt, a new generation of Israelites finally crossed the Jordan River and entered the promised land of Canaan. Centuries followed in which God continued to show the people his love, while their love for him ebbed and flowed.

In Psalm 136, the persistent love of God forms a refrain against the sweep of Israel's early history. Read through Psalm 136. What events have demonstrated the faithful love of God?

_____

_____

_____

_____

BETROTHED TO THE LORD FOREVER

After the reign of King David, the nation of Israel split into two kingdoms: a northern kingdom (Israel) and a southern kingdom (Judah). Two series of kings led the nations, sometimes into idolatry and sometimes into repentance and righteousness. When the people fell into idolatry, the Lord sent prophets to try to bring them back to himself.

During the eighth century B.C. the Lord sent the prophet Hosea with a message of judgment and, ultimately, one of deep, steadfast love. Hosea started out with a tough assignment. In a shocking demand, God told Hosea, "Go, marry a promiscuous woman and have children with her, for like an adulterous wife this land is guilty of unfaithfulness to the LORD" (Hosea 1:2). Hosea therefore married an immoral woman named Gomer. She had several children with different men. The marriage of Gomer and Hosea gave a picture of the relationship between Israel and the Lord.

Read Hosea 2–3.

In what ways did Israel's behavior resemble that of an unfaithful spouse?

_____

_____

_____

_____

After a time of judgment, how did God promise to ultimately respond to the nation of Israel?

_____

_____

_____

_____

Read Hosea 11:1-11. What yearning words and phrases does the Lord use to express his steadfast love?

_____

_____

_____

_____

One scholar notes that Hosea 11:1-4, 7-9 is "the nearest the OT approaches to a declaration that God is love."[1] Yet the book of Hosea does not even begin to say everything about the loving nature of God in the Old Testament. God consistently made his love known in verbal announcements through his prophets and in his protection and discipline of Israel.

Ultimately God showed the full extent of his love, not only for Israel but for the whole world, in Jesus Christ: "For God so loved the world that he gave his one and only Son, that whoever believes in him shall not perish but have eternal life. For God did not send his Son into the world to condemn the world, but to save the world through him" (John 3:16-17).

WHAT ABOUT GOD'S WRATH?

Remember our friend who said, "God in the New Testament is loving, but God in the Old Testament was terrible"? She was thinking of the many Old Testament expressions of God's fiery judgment against sin.

God's love and God's wrath are both obvious in Scripture. Our human minds and hearts struggle to reconcile the two, however.

Yet even in the sternest judgments against his people, God revealed his steadfast love and mercy. When the northern kingdom of Israel and the southern kingdom of Judah were each conquered (at different times) by foreign powers and taken into exile, God made it clear that the conquests happened because the people ignored his warnings and persisted in idolatry, worshiping false gods instead of the one true God. (See 2 Kings 17:7-23 and 2 Chronicles 36:15-21.) In the midst of Judah's unfaithfulness and idolatry, the prophet Habakkuk prayed to the Lord, "In wrath remember mercy" (Habakkuk 3:2), and the Lord answered his prayer. In the midst of the destruction of Jerusalem by the Babylonians, the Lord sent a promise of mercy through the prophet Jeremiah.

This is the word that came to Jeremiah from the LORD: "This is what the LORD, the God of Israel, says: 'Write in a book all the words I have spoken to you. The days are coming,' declares the LORD, 'when I will bring my people Israel and Judah back from captivity and restore them to the land I gave their ancestors to possess,' says the LORD." (Jeremiah 30:1-3)

Later God again reiterated his love through Jeremiah: "The LORD appeared to us in the past, saying: 'I have loved you with an everlasting love; I have drawn you with loving-kindness'" (Jeremiah 31:3).

In addition to idolatry, failure to care for the poor and show justice caused God to become angry with Israel. We would not think much of a God who failed to care about suffering and injustice; God's anger flashes out against people who use and abuse others, as Israel was doing. Yet, even in the midst of his anger, we see evidence of his love.

Read Isaiah 59. At whom is God angry, and why?

_____

_____

_____

_____

What action does he ultimately take?

_____

_____

_____

_____

God's wrath, then, defends and protects those he loves. In the passages we looked at, his wrath essentially brought justice for the poor and suffering and saved the Israelites—much of the generation that was living as well as future generations—from the lasting, destructive practices of idolatry. In essence, his wrath exists because he knows that the life he calls people to is the one that's best (safest, most caring, most loving, most full of goodness, etc.) for everyone, and that disobedience to him always causes pain in some way for someone.

Throughout the Old Testament, God showed his love in various ways. John now writes that God has shown his love in the ultimate way: "This is how God showed his love among us: He sent his one and only Son into the world that we might live through him. This is love: not that we loved God, but that he loved us and sent his Son as an atoning sacrifice for our sins" (1 John 4:9-10). The "atoning sacrifice" is the death of Jesus Christ on the cross. God accepts the sacrifice of Jesus as full payment of the just penalty for our sins.

We can imagine no more terrible outpouring of wrath than the violent death of God's own Son. We can imagine no more lavish display of love than the mercy which God extends to us through the cross. In the cross, God's wrath and God's love meet to accomplish reconciliation between God and humanity.

LOVE ONE ANOTHER

John says that the natural result of God's overwhelming love for us is that we will love each other: "Dear friends, since God so loved us, we also ought to love one another" (v. 11). The idea did not originate with John. Just as God's love for humanity is an Old Testament concept, so is God's command for people to love one another. The two ideas are inseparable in the Old Testament.

Buried in a list of brief commands in Leviticus is the little statement "Love your neighbor as yourself" (Lev 19:18). It is easy to overlook, yet Jesus revealed its importance when he put it alongside the great *Shema* of Deuteronomy 6:5 in answer to a question from an expert in the Jewish law about which commandment was the greatest. Jesus quoted the *Shema*—"Love the Lord your God with all your heart and with all your soul and with all your mind"—and called it "the first and greatest commandment." Then he immediately quoted Leviticus 19:18: "And the second is like it: 'Love your neighbor as yourself.' All the Law and the Prophets hang on these two commandments" (Matthew 22:37-40).

Read Leviticus 19:18 and fill in the blanks for the following sentence:

The contrast that's set up in this commandment is between _____ and _____.

What do you think it means to "love your neighbor as yourself"?

_____

_____

_____

_____

How does the closing statement "I am the LORD" intensify this commandment?

_____

_____

_____

_____

The love commanded in the law of God was as radical and countercultural then as it is today. In the violent milieu of Old Testament times, injury called for an escalating cycle of blood revenge. Moshe Greenberg explains, "In societies that lack a strong central authority the defense of private property and life is the task of the kinship group. . . . If a person is slain, his kin take vengeance for him upon the slayer, or on one or more of the slayer's kinship group. This in turn may give rise to countervengeance, and a blood feud, terminating at times only with the extinction of a family, is set in motion."[2] Israel's law called for equitable punishment which fairly fit the crime—usually restitution for wrongs done. Leviticus 24:19-20 states: "Anyone who injures their neighbor is to be injured in the same manner: fracture for fracture, eye for eye, tooth for tooth. The one who has inflicted the injury must suffer the same injury." Scholars point out that "although this may seem extreme, it in fact limits the punishment that can be inflicted on the person accused of the injury."[3]

In addition, the law laid out a system where every seven years all debts were to be cancelled and all indentured servants were to be set free (Deuteronomy 15). As David Lamb writes, "Compared to other ancient Near Eastern literature, the Old Testament is shockingly progressive in its portrayals of divine love, acceptance of foreigners and affirmation of women."[4]

Addressing people who were very familiar with God's law, Jesus set forth an even more radical picture of God's love. Read Matthew 5:21-22, 27-30. How do Jesus' strong words show his profound concern for how people treat each other?

_____

_____

_____

_____

LOVE MADE VISIBLE

"Why can't we see God?" a sixth-grader asked us recently. While we could answer by explaining that God is a spirit, Scripture offers an additional perspective.

Compare these two Scripture passages:

No one has ever seen God, but the One and Only, who is at the Father's side, has made him known. (John 1:18)

No one has ever seen God; but if we love one another, God lives in us and his love is made complete in us. (1 John 4:12)

What do these two statements tell you about how people today can see God?

_____

_____

_____

_____

For a few precious years on earth, some people *did* see God incarnate in Christ. John called Jesus "that which was from the beginning, which we have heard, which we have seen with our eyes, which we have looked at and our hands have touched" (1 John 1:1). Similarly, the Gospel of John reports that "we have seen his glory, the glory of the one and only Son, who came from the Father, full of grace and truth" (John 1:14). If we want to see God, we must look at Jesus and we must love each other. When those things happen, love becomes visible, and God can be seen by mortal human beings.

---

[1]F. H. Palmer, "Love, Beloved," in *New Bible Dictionary*, ed. I. Howard Marshall, A. R. Millard, J. I. Packer and D. J. Wiseman, 3rd ed. (Downers Grove, IL: InterVarsity Press, 1996), p. 700.

[2]Moshe Greenberg, "Avenger of Blood," in *Interpreter's Dictionary of the Bible*, ed. George Arthur Buttrick (Nashville: Abingdon Press, 1962), 1:321.

[3]John H. Walton, Victor H. Matthews and Mark W. Chavalas, *The IVP Bible Background Commentary: Old Testament* (Downers Grove, IL: InterVarsity Press, 2000), p. 139.

[4]David Lamb, *God Behaving Badly: Is the God of the Old Testament Angry, Sexist and Racist?* (Downers Grove, IL: InterVarsity Press, 2011), p. 23.

PART 3. REFLECT
Love's Evidence
(On Your Own)

When Laura Ingalls was growing up in various places in the American frontier—Wisconsin, Oklahoma, Minnesota and the Dakota Territory—she wanted nothing more than to be outdoors working or playing. She cheerfully helped with harvesting, gardening and caring for the animals.

During the Ingalls' time in western Minnesota, scarlet fever struck most of the family. The disease left Laura's older sister Mary completely blind. Mary had to give up her dream of being a teacher. She was still quite capable of doing housework and sewing, though, jobs she had enjoyed even before she lost her sight. Laura often resented Mary because Mary was so *good*. She was always gentle, patient and uncomplaining. Sometimes Laura wanted to slap Mary for all her perfection.

After the Ingalls family moved west to the Dakota Territory, a minister told them of a college for the blind in Iowa. College was an impossible dream for Mary unless the family could raise a substantial amount of money. The only way Laura could contribute was to do something that went against all her wishes. She could become what Mary had wanted to be—a teacher. If Laura did well in school for the next two years, at age sixteen she could get a teaching certificate.

Laura didn't want to teach school. The last thing she wanted was to stay indoors and study just so she could eventually stay indoors and teach.

Laura relented, however, because of her maturing attitude toward her sister. On one of their walks, Laura realized that she was changing. She began to admire Mary. As the possibilities rose that Mary could leave for college, Laura realized how much she would miss her. She found she loved Mary after all.

Laura's first teaching job was at a tiny new school twelve long wintery miles from home.

Laura boarded in a tiny shanty with a couple who could barely tolerate each other. The man was nearly silent. The woman hated the isolated pioneer life and had become unbalanced. She resented Laura's presence, screamed at her husband and threatened him with a butcher knife. Laura's only refuge was the schoolhouse. Though her students were difficult and she often felt like a failure, being at school was better than being at the shanty.

Back at home on weekends, Laura admitted to her younger sister Carrie how much she hated teaching. She didn't tell her parents because she was afraid they would make her quit before the year was out. Instead, she doggedly kept at it. What mattered was what was best for Mary. Laura's pay was enough to keep Mary in college that year and to bring her home the next summer. Only Laura Ingalls's love for her sister kept her in that first teaching job. Love led her to sacrifice her own ideal plans for Mary's sake.

In creation and in his Word, God offers us testimony of his love for us. But John says that God has done even more. He has made the ultimate sacrifice: "This is how God showed his love among us: He sent his one and only Son into the world that we might live through him. This is love: not that we loved God, but that he loved us and sent his Son as an atoning sacrifice for our sins" (1 John 4:9-10).

If God has gone to the ultimate lengths of love for us, we can only respond by making tangible sacrifices of love for one another. We may express our love in words, but our words are empty if they are not accompanied by actions. We may have warm fuzzy feelings inside, but our feelings remain private pleasures if they do not translate into deeds. We are even called to love others when warm sentiments are absent. Human feelings ebb and flow. True Christian love is not a slave to such emotional fluctuations.

Ben Witherington III writes about *love* in the Scriptures:

> In the Hebrew Scriptures, *hesed* refers to a sort of love that has been promised and is owed—covenant love, that is—as in Hosea 1:1: "When Israel was a child, I loved him and out of Egypt I called my son." Covenant love is the love God promised to give to his covenant people, and which they in turn were to respond with in kind, loving the God of the Bible with all their hearts, minds and strength. . . . Covenant love, like marital love, is neither optional nor unconditional; it is obligatory. This is not to say *hesed* is compelled—just as in a marriage, love cannot be forced—but it is commanded. . . .
>
> It is sometimes difficult for a modern person, who associates love with uncontrollable feelings, to understand how the Bible can command love of God, neighbors, even enemies. But in the Bible the many terms translated as "love" do not refer primarily to feelings. They refer to decisions of the will. This voluntaristic notion of love is recalled in modern wedding services, where the bride and groom say "I do" and "I will" when they are asked to make their vows, not "I feel like it." In the Bible, when God's people are called upon to "love," they are being asked to do something loving and responsive to the love of God, whether they feel like it or not.[1]

A young couple lived next door to us, not married, each with a long history of living with various other people. One day the woman announced to us that this current guy was *the* guy for her, for the rest of her life. There would never be another in the whole world. We asked if they planned to be married. "No," she quickly responded, "a marriage is too hard to get out of. Too much red tape." Her boyfriend may have been the only guy for her, but she was already planning her exit strategy. It was no surprise when their relationship soon disintegrated.

By contrast we remember the nursing home where Sandy's mother lived for several years. Sandy's father had died several years before, but there were other residents in the nursing home whose spouses were still living. We recall a woman who arrived one day carrying balloons which proclaimed "Happy 50th!" Her husband was in the nursing home, in circumstances neither of them would have chosen. Perhaps at times he did not even recognize her. Never mind; her love overcame all that. She was determined that nothing would stop them from celebrating their fiftieth wedding anniversary.

The pure and perfect love of Jesus did not always feel good or make him happy. In the hours before he was arrested, tried and crucified, Jesus prayed in the garden of Gethsemane. He was about to give his life for the world. He was there in that place, facing that death, because he loved us. How did he *feel?* He told three of his disciples, "My soul is overwhelmed with sorrow to the point of death" (Mark 14:34). He prayed desperately to his Father, "Take this cup from me. Yet not what I will, but what you will" (Mark 14:36).

Jesus obeyed his Father when he didn't "feel like it." Because he obeyed in spite of his emotions, we are now empowered to love God and each other, as John admonishes us: "Dear children, let us not love with words or speech but with actions and in truth" (1 John 3:18).

What's the main idea in this section?

What is one thing you can act on based on this reading?

---

[1]Ben Witherington III, "From Hesed to Agape: What's Love Got to Do with It?" *Bible Review*, December 2003, accessed December 6, 2011, at www.basarchive.org/sample/bswbBrowse.asp?PubID=BSBR&Volume=19&Issue=6&ArticleID=7.

Part 4. Discuss
Putting It All Together
(With a Group)

OPEN

Complete the following sentence: I feel most loved when another person

    (a) gives me a hug

    (b) brings me a hot meal when I'm sick

    (c) really tunes in and listens to me

    (d) shares him or herself with me

    (e) gently confronts me in an area where I need help

    (f) prays with me

    (g) _____.

In groups of two or four, discuss the responses you each chose and why.

READ 1 JOHN 4:7-16.

The word *love* (or some form of it) is mentioned sixteen times in 1 John 4. From the Christian point of view, we must wonder what this thing called love is, how we get it and how we can give it away to others who need it.

1. Verses 9-10 say that Christ's incarnation and death show us God's love. How do these two events help you to understand God's love?

2. The "Connect: Scripture to Scripture" section offered evidence that the God of the Old Testament is the God of love. What is significant about the reasons God gave for choosing Israel as his people?

3. Many people see a contradiction between God's love for humanity and God's wrath against sin. How can you reconcile the two?

4. What ideas in parts two and three clarified or changed your understanding of love?

5. John writes that "everyone who loves has been born of God and knows God" (v. 7) and "whoever lives in love lives in God, and God in him" (v. 16). We have all noticed that sometimes non-Christians act in more loving ways than Christians act. How do you account for this apparent inconsistency?

6. For whom do you find it easiest to make sacrifices, and for whom do you find it most difficult? Why?

7. Suppose another Christian observed you speaking or acting in a particularly unloving manner. What would you want that person to do? What would you want that person *not* to do?

8. Think of someone you find hard to love. What is it in *yourself* (rather than in the other person) which makes it difficult to love that person?

9. John writes that "love comes from God" (v. 7). Perhaps sometimes you've found that you lack love, and you have realized that you have lost your close connection with God. At such times, how have you re-kindled your love for God?

10. Where do you think God wants you to put love into action this week? Focus on two or three situations.

11. How can you remind each other to carry through with your plans to put love into action?

Pray together for the courage to sacrifice for others. Thank God for the ultimate sacrifice of Jesus Christ, his beloved Son.

SESSION TWO

JOY

Luke 24:33-53

WHERE WE'RE GOING

Part 1. Investigate: Luke 24:33-53 (On Your Own)

Part 2. Connect: Scripture to Scripture (On Your Own)

Part 3. Reflect: Joy in Unexpected Places (On Your Own)

Part 4. Discuss: Putting It All Together (With a Group)

A PRAYER TO PRAY

Here's a prayer you can use to set you on your way:

Lord Jesus, when your disciples were at their point of deepest despair, you suddenly stood among them and overwhelmed them with joy. We are bold to ask that you would do the same for us. Remind us that whether our circumstances are easy or difficult, you stand in our midst. Forgive us for not letting your joy flow through us to others. Make us people who are more free to show our joy. We pray this in the name of our risen Savior, Jesus. Amen.

PART 1. INVESTIGATE
Luke 24:33-53

Read Luke 24:33-53.

1. What progression in the disciples' understanding do you notice in this passage?

2. Try to picture those first few moments when the two find the eleven and the others (vv. 33-35). Describe what you see and hear.

24:36-38. *Because the resurrection of all the dead had not yet occurred, the disciples think Jesus might be a "ghost" or some other spirit. On the popular level, some people held a belief in ghosts without considering that it contradicted the idea of afterlife in paradise or hell (Gehenna) and the doctrine of the bodily resurrection. But Jesus assures them that he is not an example of a ghost but of the bodily resurrection.*

3. Suddenly something happens to interrupt the story (vv. 36-39). How does the climate in the room change? Why?

4. How did it help the disciples for Jesus to show them his hands and feet, and ask them to touch him (vv. 39-40)?

5. In what ways would the disciples' faith in Jesus have been increased by seeing him eat (vv. 41-43)?

6. Think about your wildest dream coming true. How does this help you understand what it meant for the disciples to be too joyful and amazed to believe (v. 41)?

7. When is it hard for you to believe Jesus is real?

8. Why were these activities—showing them his hands and feet and eating before them—necessary before he could open their minds to understand the Scriptures (v. 45)?

9. The disciples, along with almost all other Jews, expected that the Messiah would be a political conqueror who would stamp out Rome's rule and restore Israel to her former glory. How does Jesus change their vision and understanding at this point in the narrative (vv. 46-47)?

10. What the Father has promised (v. 49) is the Holy Spirit who would be sent to the disciples in the near future. In light of what Jesus has just been saying (vv. 46-48), why is the Spirit's presence so important?

11. In verses 52-53 the disciples have changed from wondering and disbelieving to having "great joy." How does Jesus' resurrection and the promise of the Holy Spirit help you to define *joy*?

12. How is Christian joy different from the happiness we get from the special events of our lives?

Spend time now praising God for who he is and what he has done for us.

24:44-46. *Other Jewish writings mention the threefold division of the Old Testament. Jewish interpreters sometimes spoke of God "opening their eyes" to his truths, language with Old Testament precedent (Ps 119:18). Although the Gospels report Jesus' disagreement with his contemporaries on many issues, every stratum of Gospel tradition reports his appeal to the Old Testament to define his mission. Although he may have disagreed with many of his contemporaries on Old Testament interpretation, he agrees with them concerning its authority.*

24:47-49. *Isaiah spoke of Israel being witnesses to (or against) all the nations in the end time (43:10; 44:8), by means of the endowment of the Spirit (42:1; 44:3). The Spirit was especially associated with the ability to prophesy, to speak as God inspired a person to speak.*

THOUGHTS FROM HAZEL

My father was dying. He had been sick for a long time. As he lay in a coma, I held his hand with my left one while writing out the answers to this study on joy with my right hand. It was Tuesday; on Thursday I was supposed to lead our small group study on joy. However, the next day (Wednesday), my dear daddy went to be with the Lord—the risen Lord Jesus about whom I had written this study and on whom I had just been preparing to lead my small group.

Needless to say, I didn't lead the study on Thursday. I did grieve for Daddy. But oh—how joy also filled my heart and soul! Jesus was and is alive! The disciples saw him. And now my own father was in heaven seeing him too!

At the funeral, a dear friend sang in a clear soprano voice the words of an old hymn: "When we all get to heaven, what a day of rejoicing that will be! When we all see Jesus, we'll sing and shout the victory!"

In question six you were asked to get in touch with your wildest dreams. If we are Christians, seeing Jesus will indeed be the answer to our wildest dream, as it was for the disciples in Luke 24.

PART 2. CONNECT
Scripture to Scripture

THE GOD OF JOY

From the very beginning, joy runs throughout the Old Testament. God himself is the God of joy. When he had finished making everything, "God saw all that he had made, and it was very good" (Genesis 1:31). Though the word *joy* is not overtly stated, we can sense God's pleasure and satisfaction as he regarded his completed work of creation.

How do you respond to the idea that God took pleasure and rejoiced in his own creation?

___ It's hard to grasp. I usually think of God as grouchy or at least stern.

___ I believe that God rejoiced and still rejoices over his creation.

___ It's a new idea to me, but it makes sense.

___ Another response: _____

GOD AS THE SOURCE OF JOY

The nation of Israel was enslaved in Egypt for four hundred years before they were freed under the leadership of Moses and Aaron. While they were still in the wilderness en route to the land of Canaan, God established the ways they should worship him together. Included in their yearly gatherings was the Feast of Tabernacles.

Read the instructions for the Feast of Tabernacles in Deuteronomy 16:13-15. This feast was to take place in the seventh month of the Hebrew religious calendar, corresponding to September-October in our calendar. What reasons were the Israelites given for rejoicing?

_____

_____

_____

_____

Read further instructions about the Feast of Tabernacles in Leviticus 23:33-43. Why would living in temporary shelters during this week intensify their reasons for rejoicing?

_____

_____

_____

_____

Scholars note that in the Hebrew language the verb for "to rejoice" most often "refers to a spontaneous emotion or extreme happiness which is expressed in some visible and/or external manner. It does not normally represent an abiding state of well-being or feeling."[1] This seems counter to the common contrast between *joy* and *happiness*. Happiness is seen as being tied to immediate, temporary circumstances. Everybody feels happy when things go well (except for die-hard pessimists), and everybody feels down when things go badly. But if both joy and happiness are tied to circumstances, what's the difference between them?

The difference is that joy is tied to *eternal* circumstances. It is not a free-floating feeling with no basis in fact; that sort of "joy" could be induced with drugs. Rather, it finds its source in the character of God and the redemptive work of God. Joy was part of God's perfect creation before the Fall, and the Fall did not wipe it out. Thus, even in our fallen state we still can know joy because we are in relationship with God the creator.

Israel's joy at the Feast of Tabernacles arose from gratitude for God's redemption. Christians' joy arises from God's completed redemption in Christ. Our redemption is an eternal unchanging reality for which we can have unending joy.

The songs and poetry of the Psalms often ring out with joy. Read the following excerpts from the Psalms. Draw lines to match up the psalm (left column) with *who or what* is rejoicing (right column).

O LORD, the king rejoices in your strength
   How great is his joy in the victories you give! . . .
Surely you have granted him eternal blessings   the king
and made him glad with the joy of your presence. (Psalm 21:1, 6)

Clap your hands, all you nations;
   shout to God with cries of joy.
How awesome is the LORD most high,
   the great King over all the earth! (Psalm 47:1-2)

                                    all nations

Shout for joy to God, all the earth!
   Sing the glory of his name;
   make his praise glorious! (Psalm 66:1-2)

Let the heavens rejoice, let the earth be glad;
   let the sea resound, and all that is in it;
   Let the fields be jubilant, and everything in them.   all creation
Then all the trees of the forest will sing for joy;
   They will sing before the LORD, for he comes,
   he comes to judge the earth. (Psalm 96:11-13)

Shout for joy to the LORD, all the earth.   all the earth
   Worship the LORD with gladness;
   come before him with joyful songs. (Psalm 100:1-2)

The Psalms give a wide scope of *who* and *what* rejoices in God. We are included in the scope of that joy. Rewrite some of the phrases from the Psalms above, inserting your own name as one of the rejoicers. For example:

Shout for joy to God, *Dale!*

Let *Sandy* rejoice, let *Sandy* be glad.

As God was the source of Old Testament believers' joy, Jesus Christ was the source of joy for the early Christians. Read 1 Peter 1:3-9. Peter is addressing believers who have been scattered because of persecution and who now "suffer grief in all kinds of trials" (v. 6). Why are these oppressed believers still rejoicing (vv. 6, 9-10)?

GOD AS THE RESTORER OF JOY

After the exodus from Egypt, once the Israelites were established in Canaan, they developed an erratic record of faithfulness to the Lord. They would fall into idolatry, repent, return to the Lord and fall into idolatry again. Prophets saw the approaching judgment of God and tried to call the people back to repentance.

One such prophet was Zephaniah. His little book is often overlooked in the collection of Minor Prophets at the end of the Old Testament. Zephaniah prophesied in the southern kingdom of Judah during the reign of the righteous king Josiah in the seventh century B.C. The northern kingdom of Israel had been conquered a hundred years earlier, but Judah had been spared at that time. Judah's reprieve, Zephaniah warned, was about to end.

Read Zephaniah 3:1-8. It is hard to see any room for joy in the midst of all this judgment. Then abruptly the mood of Zephaniah's prophecy changes. Read Zephaniah 3:9-20.

What does the Lord promise to accomplish for Israel?

_____

_____

_____

_____

Which parts of this passage make you wish you could put yourself down right in the middle of the action, and why?

_____

_____

_____

_____

Write out verse 17 word for word. How will God himself join in the people's restored joy?

_____

_____

_____

_____

_____

_____

The Jews had already spent years in exile when the Persian Empire took ascendancy over Babylonia. Almost overnight, by the hand of God, the fortunes of the Jews changed. Cyrus king of Persia decreed that they could go back to their homeland. They returned in several waves of repatriation. But there were problems. Their temple and the walls of Jerusalem were in ruins, and so was the people's knowledge of God's law.

Under the leadership of Nehemiah and Zerubbabel, the walls of Jerusalem and the temple were rebuilt. The priest Ezra arrived from Babylon to teach the people the law of God, which had been neglected for years.

Read Nehemiah 8. Picture these events as an unfolding series of dramatic scenes. What is the central action of each scene?

Scene 1: vv. 1-3

Scene 2: vv. 4-8

Scene 3: vv. 9-12

Scene 4: vv. 13-15

Scene 5: vv. 16-18

Paraphrase Nehemiah's statement "Do not grieve, for the joy of the LORD is your strength" (Nehemiah 8:10).

_____

_____

_____

_____

The Israelites renewed the celebration of the Feast of Tabernacles even while Ezra continued to read from the law of God (Nehemiah 8:18). Review what you read about the Feast of Tabernacles in Leviticus 23:33-43 and Deuteronomy 16:13-15. Why is it especially appropriate that the Israelites should re-establish the Feast of Tabernacles at this point?

_____

_____

_____

_____

Almost six hundred years after Nehemiah and Ezra, Jesus the Messiah was born. Read Luke 1:46-55, Mary's response when she learned that she would give birth to the Savior. Mary felt joy, and she used words which show that her joy was meant to extend beyond herself. Who else does she say will be included in the joyful blessings of God?

_____

_____

_____

_____

God had long promised through his prophets that Israel's time of repentance and mourning over their sin would end and their joy would be restored. There was partial fulfillment of that joy at the time of Nehemiah. When Christ came, the more complete fulfillment of joy became possible. The disciples got a taste of it when Jesus rose from the dead and "they still did not believe it because of joy and amazement" (Luke 24:41). Our full perfection of joy, of course, will have to wait until Christ returns in triumph.

LUKE 24 AND FULFILLED PROPHECIES

Prophecies about the Messiah. In Luke 24:44-45 Jesus tells his disciples that "'everything must be fulfilled that is written about me in the Law of Moses, the Prophets and the Psalms.' Then he opened their minds so they could understand the Scriptures." Following are a few of the Messianic prophecies from Moses, the Prophets and the Psalms which Jesus likely explained to his disciples. How do you see Jesus Christ in each of these passages?

Deuteronomy 18:15-19 (Moses speaking to the Israelites in the desert):

Isaiah 11:

Psalm 22:

Prophecies about Israel's witness to the world. Jesus next told his disciples that "repentance and the forgiveness of sins will be preached in his name to all nations, beginning at Jerusalem. You are witnesses of these things" (Luke 24:47-48). God never meant for his redemption to stay the exclusive property of the Jewish nation. Israel was to be a witness to all nations. God said through the prophet Isaiah that his Messiah would be "a light for the Gentiles, that you may bring my salvation to the ends of the earth" (Isaiah 49:6). Now the disciples would begin to carry that light outward with Jerusalem as their base. David Pao and Eckhard Schnabel explain:

The notion that the beginning of the messianic age will be noticeable first in Jerusalem, where the good news of repentance and the forgiveness of sins is first proclaimed (24:47), indicates a reversal of the direction assumed by the OT promises concerning the conversion of the Gentiles in the last days (Isa. 2:2-5 [Mic. 4:1-4]; 14:2; 45:14; 49:22-23; 55:5; 66:20; Jer. 16:19-21; Zeph. 3:9-10; Zech. 8:20-23; 14:16-19). Whereas the Jews expected the nations to come from "outside" to Jerusalem as the center of the world, Jesus tells his disciples that they will begin in Jerusalem and then move out to the nations.[2]

Imagine that you are one of the disciples in that room. When you hear Jesus say "repentance and the forgiveness of sins will be preached in his name to all nations, beginning at Jerusalem," what goes through your mind?

_____

_____

_____

_____

What do you think when Jesus adds, "You are witnesses of these things"?

Prophecies about the Holy Spirit. The disciples may have been impatient to start out on their mission, but Jesus restrained them. He gave them a promise and instructions which must have sounded mysterious: "I am going to send you what my Father has promised; but stay in the city until you have been clothed with power from on high" (Luke 24:49).

The promise for which they waited was the gift of the Holy Spirit. The Spirit had been promised long before this, including in the following Scriptures. According to these passages, what kind of power does the Holy Spirit bring?

Isaiah 44:1-5:

Joel 2:28-32:

What reasons do these fulfilled prophecies give for God's people (including us now) to rejoice?

_____

_____

_____

_____

[1]W. E. Vine, Merrill F. Unger and William White Jr., "To Rejoice," in *Vine's Complete Expository Dictionary of Old and New Testament Words* (Nashville: Thomas Nelson, 1996), p. 196.

[2]David W. Pao and Eckhard J. Schnabel, "Luke," in *Commentary on the Old Testament Use of the New Testament*, ed. G. K. Beale and D. A. Carson (Grand Rapids: Baker Academic, 2007), p. 401.

PART 3. REFLECT
Joy in Unexpected Places

Shortly after the breakup of the Soviet Union, we taught English at a university in Ukraine. We had spent two years living overseas some twenty years before and we always wanted to have the experience again. At last the opportunity was ours.

Because of our previous time overseas, we felt reasonably well equipped to deal with living in a foreign country. The prospect of figuring out the trains, living in spartan conditions and eating unfamiliar food did not intimidate us.

What did intimidate us was the task of teaching English to university students, especially students who were studying to become English teachers. We were not professional English teachers ourselves. In fact, we were not professional teachers of any kind. And we were not certified in English as a Second Language. Our organization, TeachOverseas, provided six weeks of training, but as the plane took off from New York, we wondered if we would be up to the demands of teaching.

During that year our expectations got turned upside down. Living conditions were difficult, as we were bounced from a room in a tiny house to a rat-and-bedbug-infested dormitory and finally to a clean but barren apartment. Our school administration went out of their way to make us feel unwanted and unneeded. We went for four months without being paid. We never left home without wearing backpacks because we just might see someone on the street selling something we needed, and they might not be there the next day. There was no such thing as a washing machine; we did all laundry by hand on a washboard. Electricity was chancy at the school and at home. We usually had water, although we boiled it for safety. There was one memorable ten-day period when our apartment had

only hot water, no cold.

In spite of all those hardships, during our year in Ukraine *we had joy*. Why? Because we had a strong sense of being among the right people at the right time, and of being part of what God was doing among those people after the fall of communism. The parents of our students were almost all atheists. For our students, Christian faith was something their grandparents had talked about. Now they were curious and were unafraid to ask questions. We arranged to use a room in the school on Saturdays for Bible studies, and several students came regularly. Through a visiting InterVarsity Christian Fellowship staff person, several made commitments to Christ. After we returned to the U.S., another student wrote to say he had trusted in Christ. Certainly God could have sent anyone to engage with those students, but he sent *us*, and in that joyful circumstance we felt both humbled and privileged.

Our students also brought us joy by caring for us in practical ways. For Dale's November birthday, each of our three classes threw him a surprise party (though by the third one he was no longer surprised). Most of our students always arrived for class early, greeted us with big smiles and hung around after class to ask questions about English. And if we needed something, they would try to find it for us, whether legally or—we often suspected—under the table. They brought us food. They gave us books and their own original handiwork and drawings and paintings.

One of their most mundane gifts was also the most memorable because of when it arrived. Right at New Year's we managed to move out of the dorm and into our own apartment. The kitchen had zero cookware except one kettle for boiling water. Sitting at the kitchen table that first evening, Sandy observed, "I could manage to cook most things if I just had a frying pan." What happened next sounds far-fetched, but it's true. There was a knock at the door. In walked one of our few male students, holding a frying pan! He said he had won it in some kind of contest and didn't need it, so could we use it?

Now *that* was joy, because God directly answered a rather indirect prayer and because our student cared enough to come by and give us something we might need.

By the end of our year in Ukraine we realized that teaching, the thing which had caused us the most apprehension, was the thing which had given us the most joy. We didn't cry at leaving our apartment or riding the subway for the last time, but we shed tears at the graduation ceremony for our students and as we said goodbye to each one of them.

Jesus' disciples experienced joy precisely when and where they did not expect it. When they gathered together after his death, they were not prepared for joy. They probably thought they would never rejoice about anything again. What was there to be joyful about? They had seen their Lord condemned, crucified and buried. The cause—more than that, the *person*—for whom they had given up everything was gone. As a result, their own lives were in danger, and for what?

"We had hoped that he was the one who was going to redeem Israel," mourned one of them on the road to Emmaus. Sure, some women had said that Jesus' body was missing from the tomb, and they claimed some angels had said he was alive, but how could a story like that be true?

Then came the report that Jesus himself, very much alive, had appeared to Simon! And two followers had met Jesus on the road! How could that be true?

They were all talking about it at once when Jesus himself appeared among them and greeted them with "Peace be with you" (Luke 24:36). Peace? Yes, but the overwhelming emotion in the room was *joy*, the joy of life risen out of death, hope out of despair, possibility out of impossibility.

Joy can be ours all the time, not because life is fun all the time, but because we have God's redemptive and forgiving presence all the time. It doesn't mean we will giggle and jump up and down all day. It means we will have reason to rejoice in God no matter what else is going on in our lives.

We should prepare ourselves to welcome holy joy into our lives daily, hourly, minute by minute. By God's grace, joy will come to us at the least expected times in the least expected places.

What's the main idea in this section?

What is one thing you can act on based on this reading?

PART 4. DISCUSS
Putting It All Together

OPEN

When has something so overwhelmed you with joy that you could scarcely believe it was true?

READ LUKE 24:33-53.

The Holy Spirit brings joy to every Christian. He fills our hearts with praise and thankfulness to God. Yet as you look back over the past few weeks, maybe you think you haven't been very joyful. You may wonder how you can experience this refreshing fruit of the Spirit more fully.

1. As a group, discuss your individual answers to question two from part one: Try to picture those first few moments when the two followers of Jesus find the eleven and the others (vv. 33-35). What do you see and hear?

2. From your reading in "Connect: Scripture to Scripture," what evidence did you find that God is the God of joy?

3. The Jewish people were exiled from their land because of idolatry. During their exile, God promised that he would restore their joy to them. What do both of those facts tell you about who God is?

4. The disciples were overwhelmed with joy when the risen Jesus came to them. Their joy did not fade away. Forty days later (Acts 1:3) Jesus led them out of the city and ascended back to heaven. "Then they worshiped him and returned to Jerusalem with great joy. And they stayed continually at the temple, praising God" (Luke 24:52-53). Complete the following sentence with your own thoughts, and then discuss your answers as a group:

   When Jesus physically left his disciples, we might expect them to be devastated because

   _____; but instead they were joyful

   because _____.

5. When have you found it to be true that "the joy of the LORD is your strength" (Nehemiah 8:10)?

6. What do you think are your biggest barriers to joy? (Instead of looking at outward circumstances for your answer, look inside yourself, at your own attitudes.)

7. How do you react to the idea that a Christian can know joy all the time?

8. When has God brought you joy in a place or time when you were least expecting it, as was recounted in part three?

9. The disciples rejoiced because Jesus was alive. In your own life what is the connection between Jesus' resurrection and joy?

10. The disciples rejoiced after Jesus told them they were his witnesses and promised them the Holy Spirit. Think of times when the Holy Spirit has helped you bear witness to Jesus. To what extent did you know joy in that experience?

11. We are told that the disciples "stayed continually at the temple, praising God" (Luke 24:53). Think about whether you usually experience joy in corporate worship. Why do you (or why don't you) have joy at those times?

Pray for each other, that God will make you consistently joyful people.

SESSION THREE

Peace

Isaiah 43:1-7

Where We're Going

Part 1. Investigate: Isaiah 43:1-7 (On Your Own)

Part 2. Connect: Scripture to Scripture (On Your Own)

Part 3. Reflect: The God of Peace (On Your Own)

Part 4. Discuss: Putting It All Together (With a Group)

A Prayer to Pray

Here's a prayer you can use to set you on your way:

God of peace, I know that within you is no confusion or uncertainty. You have brought me safely through deep waters and raging fires, and you will do it again. You have reconciled me to yourself and made peace through the death of your Son. Yet I confess that often I do not feel peace within myself, and I do not always live in peace with other people, especially those closest to me. Therefore I ask that your peace will replace my anxiety and that your assurance will replace my confusion. I ask this not merely so that I will feel better, but so that you will be honored and so that others will be drawn to you as they sense your peace residing in me. I ask this in the name of Christ who is our peace. Amen.

PART 1. INVESTIGATE
Isaiah 43:1-7

Read Isaiah 43:1-7.

1. What words and phrases indicate God's special relationship with Israel?

2. Twice God tells his people not to be afraid (vv. 1, 5). What dangers might they face (v. 2)?

3. How do you deal with the fears you face?

4. If the peace of God does not depend on freedom from adversity (v. 2), what does it depend on?

5. What role can adversity play in developing peace?

6. How do verses 3-4 foreshadow what God eventually does for his people?

7. Look at verses 5-7. What would it be like to have God act on your behalf in this way?

43:1 (cross-reference Deuteronomy 7:6-11). *The terminology . . . of love, loyalty and obedience ["you are mine"] is common to the international treaties of [the ancient Near East]. Hittite, Akkadian, Ugaritic and Aramaic examples all show that the positive action of the suzerain [lord] toward the vassal is expressed as love, kindness and graciousness, and in return the vassal is expected to respond with obedience and loyalty.*

43:3 (cross-reference Exodus 3:13-15). *The personal name of Israel's God, Yahweh (usually rendered LORD, as here), is built from the Hebrew verb "to be." . . . The name Yahweh for the Israelite God is attested outside the Old Testament in the Mesha Inscription, the Arad Ostraca, the Lachish letters and inscriptions from Khirbet el-Qom and Kuntillat Ajrud, to name a few of the more prominent places.*

43:3. *The Persians successfully invaded Egypt and gained control of Cush (Nubia) during the reign of Cyrus's successor, Cambyses. Seba's location is disputed.*

8. If you knew nothing about God except what you learned from this passage, what would you find him to be like?

9. What relation do you see between knowing who God is and being able to receive the peace he offers?

10. Think of the most significant human being in your life, someone you love, trust and understand (and who understands you). How did you get to know this person so intimately?

In what similar ways can you get to know God?

11. Consider the things you are anxious about currently. How can knowing God intimately produce his Spirit's peace in you?

Thank God for the aspects of his character you have seen revealed in this passage. Ask him to bring you peace in the parts of your life where you feel anxiety.

THOUGHTS FROM HAZEL

Dave and I, along with our son Kevin and his wife, Amy, had been invited one summer night to dinner at the home of friends who live several miles from us. Just as we were ready to leave, the phone rang. It was our host. "Don't come!" he shouted. "Turn on your TV. A tornado is headed straight for your town!"

At that very moment our city's siren went off. Since the siren only sounds in times of imminent danger, we knew we needed to find a safe place.

We all went to the basement and stood against the stone wall. Dave had grabbed a flashlight and portable radio, so when the lights went out we at least had a bit of light and communication with the outside world. "The tornado is directly over Urbana right now," the weather forecaster on the radio informed us. Outside, there was an eerie calm; not a leaf was moving. It was scary!

As I recall, it was Amy who led us in prayer while we waited. Since it hadn't been long since I wrote this study on peace, the words of Isaiah came back to me: "Do not fear, for I have redeemed you; I have summoned you by name; you are mine. When you pass through the waters, I will be with you; and when you pass through the rivers, they will not sweep over you. When you walk through the fire, you will not be burned; the flames will not set you ablaze. For I am the LORD your God." Nothing specifically about tornadoes, but it's certainly a paean of praise to our God for his watchful care over his children. The fruit of peace enveloped me; in the place of fear, there was serenity.

It wasn't too long before the "all clear" was announced on our little radio. The tornado had passed us. But it had touched down just half a mile or so from us and had damaged many houses. I'm not at all suggesting, of course, that people in those houses didn't pray, or that the Offner family had some kind of power over a violent storm. The point is simply that, fresh as I was from writing this study, God brought the Isaiah passage to mind at just the right time. And the fruit of his Spirit, peace, overshadowed my fears.

PART 2. CONNECT
Scripture to Scripture

ORIGINAL PEACE

When God first created the world, peace prevailed. The first human beings enjoyed peace with one another and with the rest of creation because they enjoyed peace with their Creator. Adam and Eve enjoyed such intimacy with the Lord that they were accustomed to hearing him "walking in the garden in the cool of the day" (Genesis 3:8).

Read Genesis 2:4-25. Identify all the ways you see evidence of peace in the description of Eden.

_____

_____

_____

_____

In drawings or words, express when and where have you felt the deepest sense of peace.

Why do you think you experienced such peace in that time and place?

_____

_____

_____

_____

Read Genesis 3:1-24. Identify all the ways you see evidence of peace disrupted.

_____

_____

_____

_____

Sketch some of the things (either literally or symbolically) that typically disrupt your peace.

Why do you think it is hard to maintain your peace in the midst of those disruptions?

_____

_____

_____

_____

The original peace of Eden was gone. Humanity's situation was grim—but not hopeless. While perfect peace was lost, a vestige of it remained on earth.

In the Old Testament, "peace" is expressed by the familiar Hebrew word *shalom,* which is still used as a greeting among Hebrew-speaking people. Throughout the Old Testament, shalom is experienced in several ways.

SHALOM IN A TIME OF DANGER

Isaiah 43:3 alludes to the exodus in the names of God that are used and in the mention of Egypt (v. 3). As Alec Motyer notes, "The titles of the Lord in verse 3ab flow naturally into a reference back to the exodus: because he is Yahweh, Israel's God and Holy One, their Savior, he actually did give Egypt as their ransom. Faced with Egyptian intransigent refusal to let the people go, the Lord, so to speak, weighed up whether he was prepared to shatter Egypt in order to free Israel. There was 'no contest,' and it was 'at the expense of' . . . Egypt that Israel was freed."[1]

The Israelites could look back and celebrate God's saving work during the exodus, but it was incredibly stressful for them while it was happening.

Read Exodus 14:1-14. The Israelites, under Moses' leadership, are directed by God to camp in a perilous spot, caught between the sea and the approaching Egyptian army. Their situation would not naturally lead to feelings of peace!

How does Moses reassure them?

_____

_____

_____

_____

When have you felt caught in a similar situation with your back to the wall (or sea)? What was the "sea"?

_____

_____

_____

_____

As Moses encouraged the people to trust God, the Holy Spirit encourages us to "stand firm" and "see the deliverance the LORD will bring you." How have you experienced the peace of Christ in the midst of a difficult or even dangerous situation?

_____

_____

_____

_____

SHALOM BETWEEN GOD AND HIS PEOPLE

After the exodus, God gave the Israelites the law at Sinai—a law that included five major sacrificial offerings to be made at the tabernacle (and later at the temple in Jerusalem). One offering was the *peace offering,* also known as the *fellowship offering.* It is described in Leviticus 3:1-17 and 7:11-34. The peace offering was not a sacrifice for sin; rather it was, as scholar Richard Averbeck notes, a grateful celebratory offering for personal and community well-being.

> The distinctive nature of this offering was the communal celebration of the worshipers occasioned by the sharing in the meat of the offering. It was a "fellowship," or "communion," offering that indicated and enacted the fact that there was "peace" between God and his people and that the person, family or community was, therefore, in a state of "well-being." This is why the peace offering was always the last offered when it was presented in series with other kinds of offerings.[2]

R. Laird Harris and Ronald Youngblood similarly note:

> Two basic ideas are included in this offering: peace and fellowship. The traditional translation is "peace offering," a name that comes from the Hebrew word for the offering, which in turn is related to the Hebrew word *shalom,* meaning "peace" or "wholeness." Thus the offering perhaps symbolized peace between God and man as well as the inward peace that resulted. The fellowship offering was the only sacrifice of which the offerer might eat a part. Fellowship was involved because the offerer, on the basis of the sacrifice, had fellowship with God and with the priest, who also ate part of the offering ([Lev] 7:14-15, 31-34). This sacrifice—along with others—was offered by the thousands during the three annual festivals in Israel (see Ex 23:14-17; Nu 29:39) because multitudes of people came to the temple to worship and share in a communal meal.[3]

Note that the Lord initiated this fellowship meal as part of the law he gave to Moses. What significance do you see in the fact that the offerer shared in eating this meal of peace?

_____

_____

_____

_____

There were certain points in the Israelites' history when the practice of the peace offering was particularly important and weighty. One of those times was during the reign of King Hezekiah. The king before him, King Ahaz of Judah, gave up on the Lord and turned to false gods for help during a time of national danger. He closed up the temple and set up pagan altars all over Jerusalem. The feast of Passover fell by the wayside because there were not enough faithful priests in the land and because the people were not bothering to travel to Jerusalem for the feast. When King Hezekiah took the throne, however, he restored the worship of the Lord. The temple service was reestablished, and Judah celebrated a Passover such as had never been celebrated before. In addition to Passover, they celebrated the peace offering.

> Hezekiah spoke encouragingly to all the Levites, who showed good understanding of the service of the LORD. For the seven days they ate their assigned portion and offered fellowship offerings and praised the LORD, the God of their fathers. The whole assembly then agreed to celebrate the festival seven more days; so for another seven days they celebrated joyfully. (2 Chronicles 30:22-23)

The lively celebration of those fourteen days in Jerusalem sounds more exuberant than peaceful! How would you explain the connection between *joy* and *peace?*

_____

_____

_____

_____

SHALOM BETWEEN PEOPLE AND NATIONS

Another way shalom is experienced in the Old Testament is in the absence or end of hostility between nations or clans. For example, in Deuteronomy 20:12, God instructs the Israelites to besiege any city which refuses to make peace with them. In Judges 21:13, Israel makes peace with the Benjamites, their estranged brothers, after battling them. And in 1 Chronicles 19:17-19, David overpowers the Arameans, who see the light and make peace with him.

This meaning of shalom is also used in 1 Chronicles 22:9, when King David wanted to build a permanent temple to the Lord. Read 1 Chronicles 22:5-13 and put an *x* beside any of the following statements that are true:

_____ David had compromised with his enemies too readily.

_____ David accepted the fact that Solomon would complete the temple.

_____ During Solomon's reign, Israel would be at peace with the surrounding nations.

_____ Solomon would be known as a man of war, like his father, David.

_____ David was known as a peacemaker.

Fill in the blanks for the first part of 1 Chronicles 22:9:

But you have a son who will be _____, and I will give

him _____.

INNER SHALOM

While shalom is used in Scripture to mean an absence of personal or international conflict, the biblical meaning is broader and deeper than that as well. It encompasses the ideas of *well-being* and *wholeness*. Because only God is completely whole and free from infirmity, God himself is the ultimate source of authentic shalom.

After the exodus from Egypt, Moses' brother Aaron and Aaron's sons were established as the first priests of Israel. God told them to bless the Israelites with these words:

> The LORD bless you
>   and keep you;
> the LORD make his face shine on you
>   and be gracious to you;
> the LORD turn his face toward you
>   and give you peace. (Numbers 6:24-26)

Regarding this blessing, scholar Raymond Brown notes, "Just as this priestly affirmation [Num 6:24-26] opened with a comprehensive term (*bless*), so it concludes with another Hebrew word . . . that conveys a wide range of meanings—not only health and prosperity but also well-being and inner tranquility, the serenity that comes from the assurance that God knows and supplies all that is necessary for life's journey."[4]

The prophet Isaiah referred to this kind of inner peace when he wrote:

> You will keep in perfect peace
>   him whose mind is steadfast,
>   because he trusts in you.
> Trust in the LORD forever,
>   for the LORD, the LORD himself, is the Rock eternal. (Isaiah 26:3-4)

What do you think the key words in Isaiah 26:3-4 are?

_____

_____

_____

_____

The Lord promises shalom to his forgiven people. By contrast, the stubbornly unrepentant will have no shalom.

> "I have seen his ways, but I will heal him;
>   I will guide him and restore comfort to him,
>   creating praise on the lips of the mourners of Israel.
> Peace, peace, to those far and near,"
>   says the LORD. "And I will heal them."
> But the wicked are like the tossing sea,
>   which cannot rest,
>   whose waves cast up mire and mud.
>   "There is no peace," says my God, "for the wicked." (Isaiah 57:18-21)

Fill in the blank with your personal experience:

I have found that I lose my sense of inner peace in the Lord when I _____

_____.

PEACE IS COMING

Israel could enjoy shalom in the presence of the Lord, but the world still was—and is—tainted by sin. Their prophets held out hope that a more lasting peace would come. Read Isaiah 52:7 and Nahum 1:15. The Isaiah passage is written in the context of Israel's exile to Babylon; the Nahum passage is written in the context of the fall of Israel's enemy Nineveh. What hopes will the promised messengers bring for Israel?

_____

_____

_____

_____

Read Isaiah 9:2-7. What are the characteristics of the coming one Isaiah calls the Prince of Peace (v. 6)?

_____

_____

_____

_____

Read Isaiah 11:1-9. What are the signs of peace and harmony which the Branch will bring?

_____

_____

_____

_____

Isaiah 11:9 promises peace, not because nations have solved their conflicts through diplomacy, but for what reason?

_____

_____

_____

_____

THE PEACE OF JESUS

Isaiah's prophecies about the Prince of Peace and the Branch were fulfilled in Jesus Christ. Facing crucifixion, at a time when peace seemed least likely, Jesus offered *his own* peace to his disciples. Read John 14:25-27.

What do you think are the big differences between the peace the world has to offer and the peace that Jesus offers?

_____

_____

_____

_____

_____

Where and how would you like to more profoundly experience the peace of Christ?

_____

_____

_____

_____

_____

Complete Jesus' words in verse 27:

"Peace _____ with you; my peace _____."

Notice that this is not just a far-off promise for the future but a statement of present-day reality. The Prince of Peace generously bestows his own peace on his followers.

---

[1]J. Alec Motyer, *Isaiah*, Tyndale Old Testament Commentaries (Downers Grove, IL: InterVarsity Press, 1999), pp. 302-3.

[2]Richard E. Averbeck, "Sacrifices and Offerings," in *Dictionary of the Old Testament: Pentateuch*, ed. T. Desmond Alexander and David W. Baker (Downers Grove, IL: InterVarsity Press, 2003), p. 715.

[3]R. Laird Harris and Ronald Youngblood, note on Lev 3:1, in *The NIV Study Bible*, ed. Kenneth Barker et al. (Grand Rapids: Zondervan, 1995), pp. 147-48.

[4]Raymond Brown, *The Message of Numbers*, The Bible Speaks Today (Downers Grove, IL: InterVarsity Press, 2002), p. 59.

Toward the end of his letter to the Romans, Paul gave his readers this benediction: "The God of peace be with you all" (Romans 15:33). Then, after extensive personal greetings, he assured them: "The God of peace will soon crush Satan under your feet" (Romans 16:20).

The presence of God's peace is not merely a good feeling. It has real spiritual power. It can combat the attacks of Satan.

In the previous study, we mentioned our year teaching English in Ukraine and how it was a time of profound joy. At the same time it was one of the most stressful periods of our lives. The difficulties of daily living in that time and place often left us physically exhausted. Almost everything had to be done on foot or by hand. We didn't enjoy those tasks, but we tried to look at them as challenges to be figured out and overcome.

The biggest stressors were not physical, however, but mental and emotional. Our university administration seemed to work overtime to complicate our lives. We lost our office and one of our classrooms when the school rented out the space to a bank. Several other times our classrooms and teaching schedules were abruptly changed without warning and for no apparent reason. We never knew what new situation we would encounter when we got to school; they kept us guessing all the time.

To get paid—or to try to get paid—we traveled across the city by bus and stood in line with other teachers for hours, only to be told to come back the next day, or told, "The cash drawer is empty," which actually happened once when we finally reached the front of the line.

One of the Ukrainian teachers told us bluntly, "They want to humiliate you." Perhaps the administration resented Americans being there, or perhaps there were other reasons that we never understood.

During the winter, our school suddenly closed down for several weeks because the government could not afford to heat the buildings. We did not know when or whether the school would reopen. Life in Ukraine, which had already been unpredictable, became even less predictable, if that was possible.

During this time Sandy was especially tormented by insomnia. She would lie awake at night thinking about how to solve our problems. Of course, she never came up with any solutions, and her physical and mental exhaustion the next day only worsened the stress.

Then she found one thing that gave her peace. As she lay awake, she began to silently repeat several Scriptures about peace, over and over, in the translation which was most familiar to her:

> Thou dost keep him in perfect peace,
> whose mind is stayed on thee,
> because he trusts in thee.
> Trust in the Lord forever,
> for the Lord God
> is an everlasting rock. (Isaiah 26:3-4 RSV)

> Peace I leave with you; my peace I give to you; not as the world gives do I give to you. Let not your hearts be troubled, neither let them be afraid. (John 14:27 RSV)

> I have said this to you, that in me you may have peace. In the world you have tribulation; but be of good cheer, I have overcome the world. (John 16:33 RSV)

Sandy found that if she repeated those Scriptures to herself at night, she could fall asleep more easily.

Sleeping better made her more prepared for the stresses of the next day.

There were still stresses, of course—plenty of them. Those Scriptures did not make our difficult circumstances go away. Instead they reminded Sandy of what she already knew: that no matter what was going on around her, the Lord had promised to give her peace. Even more than that, the Lord himself was with her, and he *was* her peace.

This week's Scripture from Isaiah 43 would also be good to repeat when insomnia plagues us or when we are under some other kind of emotional attack. Though this passage was written to exiles in Babylon, it is also God's Word to his people today.

Verse 1 reminds us that God is our Creator and Redeemer who knows us by name.

Verse 2 is God's promise that he will walk with us through our trials and that they will not ultimately destroy us.

Verses 3-4 assure us that God loves and values us beyond our understanding and that his purpose is to bring us to himself.

Verses 5-7 tell us not to be afraid because God has made ultimate plans for us which no one will be able to contradict.

What worries keep you awake at night? Whatever they are, God knows about them. God is bigger than those things. "The God of peace," who was there during Isaiah's time and during Paul's time, still promises to be *your* peace, today, tonight, right now.

What's the main idea in this section?

What is one thing you can act on based on this reading?

PART 4. DISCUSS
Putting It All Together

OPEN

Imagine an anxiety scale numbered 1-10 (1 = very peaceful; 10 = very anxious). How would you rate your life on this scale? Explain why you answered as you did.

READ ISAIAH 43:1-7.

Israel had sinned greatly by following other gods and by seeking alliances with heathen powers instead of resting quietly in God. This is why the people found themselves in exile in Babylon (about 540 B.C.). Isaiah 42:23-25 describes something of Israel's sin. Then Isaiah 43 begins: "But now . . ." The time of exile was almost over, and God was ready to bring his people to safety and security.

1. What specific assurances does the Lord offer his people in Isaiah 43:1-7?

2. What does the Lord specifically say about himself in this passage?

3. How would you explain the biblical meaning of *shalom* to someone unfamiliar with the word?

4. As a group, discuss your individual answers to question four from part one: What relation do you see between knowing who God is and being able to receive the peace he offers?

5. Share what you wrote down about how you usually deal with the fears you face.

6. What "waters," "rivers" or "fire" have you passed through and found that the Lord was with you?

7. In the reading, one of the authors tells how repeating Scripture gave her peace. What Scriptures have especially helped you in times of stress?

8. Based on what you've learned about peace, would you describe yourself as a peacemaker in your relationships? Why or why not?

9. What are some situations in your life that were once filled with conflict but in which the Lord brought about peace (external, internal or both)?

   How was the change from conflict to peace brought about?

10. Consider the promise that God has ultimate plans for you, as he had ultimate plans for his people in Isaiah 43:5-7. How can this assurance contribute to your sense of peace?

11. What are some current situations in which you wish you could experience the peace of God—or more of the peace of God?

Pray with and for each other about the situations you thought of in question eleven. Some situations may need to remain personal, but pray for each other to deal wisely with these situations and submit them to the God of peace.

SESSION FOUR

PATIENCE

Matthew 18:21-35

WHERE WE'RE GOING

Part 1. Investigate: Matthew 18:21-35 (On Your Own)

Part 2. Connect: Scripture to Scripture (On Your Own)

Part 3. Reflect: Is Waiting Always Patience? (On Your Own)

Part 4. Discuss: Putting It All Together (With a Group)

A PRAYER TO PRAY

Here's a prayer you can use to set you on your way:

God of mercy, through all our stubborn rebellion and thoughtless failures, you have been and continue to be patient with us. You look beyond what we are and see what we can become in you. Although we know you are patient, we get frustrated and irritated with each other and even with you. Help us to have true patience with each other. Help us to wait for your timing in every detail of life, so that we won't rush ahead of you into disaster. Thank you for your long-suffering with us. We pray this in the merciful name of Jesus. Amen.

PART 1. INVESTIGATE
Matthew 18:21-35

In Matthew 18:1 Jesus' disciples want to know who is the greatest in the kingdom of heaven. Part of Jesus' reply is that greatness in the kingdom is dependent on living a life of forgiveness and mercy.

Read Matthew 18:21-35.

1. Looking through the passage, what contrasts do you find?

2. In what ways can you identify with Peter's question (v. 21)?

3. Think about someone who has hurt you over and over. How do you feel about Jesus' answer (v. 22)?

4. Jesus' reply to Peter is enlarged by the parable in verses 23-35. What is the first servant's problem in this parable?

5. How was his problem solved far beyond anything he could have hoped for?

18:21-22. *Seventy times seven (some interpreters read seventy-seven) does not really mean exactly 490 here; it is a typically graphic Jewish way of saying "Never hold grudges." Because true repentance should involve turning from sin, some later rabbis limited opportunities for forgiveness for a given sin to three times; Peter might have thought his offer of seven times was generous.*

18:24. *Some of the disciples and perhaps Jesus himself could have smiled as the master storyteller told how far the king had let one of his servants get in debt: ten thousand talents, or "ten thousand bags of gold," probably represented more than the entire annual income of the king, and perhaps more than all the actual coinage in circulation in Egypt at the time!*

18:25. *Enslaving family members for the man's debt was a Gentile practice that the Jewish people in this period found abhorrent. "I will repay" was a standard promise in ancient business documents. But in the light of 18:24, this promise is patently impossible.*

18:28. *One hundred denarii
["a hundred silver coins"]
represented one hundred
days of a common worker's
wages, which would be a
small sum for his fellow tax
farmer, after he had finished
his accounting with the king
(18:23). It was also a
ridiculously minuscule sum
compared to what the first
servant had owed the king.
But apparently the forgiven
slave, instead of internalizing
the principle of grace, had
decided to become ruth-
lessly efficient in his exacting
of debts henceforth. Such
extreme actions as choking
are reported of angry
creditors elsewhere in
antiquity as well. Someone in
prison could not pay back
what he owed (v. 34), unless
friends came to his aid with
the requisite funds.*

18:31-33. *The king is
naturally angry; the forgiven
servant has put another of his
servants out of active
commission, hence costing
the king more lost revenues.
The king had gained more
advantage by convincing his
people of his benevolence
than he would have gained
profit from the sale of the first
servant; but once it was
rumored that this first servant,
his agent, was acting
mercilessly, it reflected badly
upon his own benevolence.*

6. How does the master illustrate God's patience and forgiveness toward us in verse 27?

7. How, specifically, does the way the first servant was treated contrast with the way he treats his fellow servant (vv. 28-30)?

8. Why do you think he failed to be patient or forgiving after having been forgiven so much?

9. If we fail to treat others with patience and forgiveness, how will God treat us (vv. 34-35)?

Why is his judgment so harsh?

10. How can a deep appreciation for God's patience and forgiveness help you to be patient with a difficult person?

18:35. *The great contrasts of the parable are humorous and effective in relaxing the ancient listener's guard, but the horrifying details of debt slavery, torture and so forth bring home the point forcefully. The story would have grabbed the ancient hearer.*

Pray that the God who has been so patient with you will help you be patient with others.

THOUGHTS FROM HAZEL

Of all the fruit of the Spirit, patience is the one that has ripened the most slowly within me. I easily get angry with people. I tend to dislike some people. It takes me a long time to forgive.

One of the things that most drives me up the wall, though, is when I'm with people and I'm "erased," by which I mean no one talks to me. I remember visiting a friend in the Chicago area one time and being taken by my hostess (along with her two little boys) to see her sister's new house. Her sister and mother were both there, but neither one spoke to me—not even to say hello. Instead they talked to the friend who brought me and to her children. I thought that complimenting something in the new house might help, so I said, "What a beautiful table!" No response; they just kept talking continuously amongst themselves. Finally, as we were getting in the car to leave, the mother—speaking to me for the first time—said, "Isn't it nice that you've had such nice *weather* while you've been here?" I reacted by waxing eloquently about the weather: "Oh yes—the blue skies, the wonderful cumulous clouds, the flowers. Oh, the beautiful pinks and yellows and blues of the flowers! And the fields covered with green beans! Just gorgeous weather!" Then we left. I don't think anyone ever caught on that I was anything but happy with the reception I'd received in that beautiful home.

But then, God's gentle, patient Spirit spoke to me, and I remembered things I'd said to people I loved that were hurtful—sometimes deliberately so. Times when I'd strongly criticized my husband or our children beyond what they deserved. Situations where I bossed people around or was aggressively confrontational. As God's fruit of patience has ripened in my life over the years, just knowing this about myself has been helpful. I have taken it to the Lord and asked him to help me hold my destructive feelings toward others compassionately. Gradually and naturally, God has helped me to become more authentic, expressive, sensitive and creative in ways that are enriching to him and to others.

And, as I've reread this passage about the unforgiving servant in Matthew 18, I have grown in my praise to the One who, though perfect, gave his very life for me on the cross—the greatest sign of his love and patience he could ever offer to me.

PART 2. CONNECT
Scripture to Scripture

GOD'S PATIENCE FROM THE BEGINNING

When Adam and Eve sinned, God could have solved the problem in several ways. He could have killed Adam and Eve and started over with newly created human beings. He could have abandoned the idea of the human race and never created any other human beings. He could have pursued some other course of action beyond our ability to imagine. Instead, he remained steadfastly committed to the human race even in their sinful state.

How does Genesis 3:21-24 demonstrate God's patience with Adam and Eve after they sinned?

_____

_____

_____

_____

Genesis 3:21-24, like Jesus' parable in Matthew 18:23-35, is essentially about forgiveness. What do you think *forgiveness* has to do with the fruit of the Spirit called *patience* in Galatians 5:22?

_____

_____

_____

_____

GOD'S PATIENCE TESTED

After the exodus from Egypt, where the Israelites had been slaves, Moses led them into the Sinai peninsula near Mt. Sinai itself, the mountain where Moses had earlier met God in the burning bush. At God's direction Moses went up the mountain to receive God's commandments.

When Moses took a long time coming back down the mountain, the people grew impatient waiting for him. They wanted gods they could see. Aaron weakened and consented to their request to make a golden calf idol with its own altar.

Of course, God knew what was going on at the foot of the mountain. He told Moses to go back down. He also told Moses what he planned to do to the rebels. Read the remarkable conversation between the Lord and Moses in Exodus 32:7-14.

Which of the following statements do you think are true, and which do you think are false?

_____ Moses was more patient than the Lord.

_____ The Lord intended to show mercy, but he wanted Moses to learn patience.

_____ The Lord was convinced by Moses' argument.

_____ The Lord was testing Moses to see if Moses could be patient with the people.

Read the continuation of the account in Exodus 32:15-20. What do you think happened to Moses' great patience? Why do you think he reacted this way?

_____

_____

_____

_____

SLOW TO ANGER

Moses came face to face with his own inadequacy to lead the people of Israel. He begged God for the assurance that he would go with them on their journey to Canaan. God answered with the promise that his presence would be with them. Then Moses, apparently caught up in the experience of speaking with God, boldly asked, "Now show me your glory" (Exodus 33:18). God told Moses that he would have to stand in a fissure in the rock for his own protection.

First, though, Moses was to chisel two new stone tablets with the commandments to replace the ones he had broken, and then carry them back up the mountain. There, while Moses huddled in a crevice in the rock, the Lord passed by, proclaiming his name: "The LORD, the LORD, the compassionate and gracious God, slow to anger, abounding in love and faithfulness, maintaining love to thousands, and forgiving wickedness, rebellion and sin. Yet he does not leave the guilty unpunished; he punishes the children and their children for the sin of the parents to the third and fourth generation" (Exodus 34:6-7).

Think about the idea that the Lord is _slow to anger_ yet at the same time _does not leave the guilty unpunished_. How would you put those ideas into your own words?

_____

_____

_____

_____

Moses and the Lord had reason to hold a similar conversation some time later. As the Israelites approached the border of Canaan, Moses sent spies ahead to reconnoiter both the fertility of the land and the strength of the native inhabitants. The spies brought back good news and bad news: the land was fruitful, but the people were powerful, living in fortified cities. In despair the Israelites made plans to return to Egypt. Moses and Aaron, however, pleaded with them to trust the Lord. The people were about to stone them when the glory of the Lord appeared at the Tent of Meeting.

Read Numbers 14:11-25. Write out word-for-word the verse in which Moses quotes back to the Lord what the Lord had said at Sinai:

_____

_____

_____

How are both of the qualities mentioned in verse 18 demonstrated by God's action in this situation?

_____

_____

_____

_____

_____

The concept that the Lord is *slow to anger* stayed with the Israelites. Read Psalm 86:14-17 and Psalm 103:6-12. What connection do you see between the Lord being slow to anger and the Lord's forgiveness?

_____

_____

_____

_____

_____

Centuries later, the Jewish people were exiled to Babylon because of their idolatry, and then were allowed to return to the land they had been promised. But when they returned, Jerusalem was in ruins. Under the leadership of Nehemiah and Ezra, the wall of Jerusalem was rebuilt and temple worship was reestablished. In addition, the Levites, who were the priests of the Lord, stood before the people and retold the history of Israel up to that point. They also led the people in confession of sin. When they reached the part where the Israelites had made the golden calf, they praised God's patience. Read Nehemiah 9:16-21.

At what points along the way had the Lord displayed patience with Israel?

_____

_____

_____

_____

_____

WAITING ON GOD

The God who is patient with humanity asks us to be patient with him. Waiting for the Lord is a common theme in the Psalms. There we find the hopes of people who are waiting for the Lord to act on their behalf, and admonitions for the reader to wait for the Lord.

Read the following passages from the Psalms. Match up each passage with the mood or circumstance of the writer.

Psalm 5:1-3   putting requests before the Lord

Psalm 27:7-14   quiet trust

Psalm 33:12-22   joyful confidence

Psalm 37:1-8   hated by enemies without reason

Psalm 38:9-16   burden of guilt over sin

Psalm 130:1-8   attacks by enemies and false witnesses

Which of these quotes from the Psalms best fits your experience right now?

_____

_____

_____

_____

In the midst of all these admonitions to wait for the Lord, it is reassuring to find the good report of one whose waiting paid off. Read Psalm 40:1-10.

About what situation in your life are verses 1-3 a description of?

_____

_____

_____

_____

David's testimony of God's faithfulness (vv. 1-10) is followed up by fresh prayers for God's help (vv. 11-17). How do you respond to the fact that David's problems were not over?

_____

_____

_____

_____

Taking Psalm 40 as a whole, what new insights does it give you about waiting for the Lord?

_____

_____

_____

_____

Esther, like David, also experienced the gratification that comes from waiting on the Lord and his timing and direction. During the time of the prophet Jeremiah, the Jews were defeated by the Babylonians and forced to live as exiles in their land. They struggled to live as God's people in an alien environment, first under the Babylonians and then under the Persians as one pagan empire replaced another (2 Chronicles 36:20-21).

At one point in the Jews' years of exile, the Persian King Xerxes I grew displeased with his queen and chose the young Jewish woman Esther as her replacement, without knowing she was Jewish. Haman, a court official and hater of the Jews, arranged for all Jewish people in the kingdom to be slaughtered on a certain upcoming day. Esther's older cousin Mordecai, who had raised her—and who had angered Haman in the first place—urged Esther to plead with the king for the lives of her people. Esther knew that approaching the king uninvited could cost her her life, but Mordecai persuaded her to do it anyway.

Read Esther 4:15–5:3.

The king offered to grant Esther anything she wanted. What a perfect opportunity to ask him to call off the planned attack on the Jews! Although Esther had been bold to enter the king's presence, she did not leap into making her appeal. Instead, she trusted God not only for *what* should happen but for *when* it should happen.

Read Esther 5:4-8. How did Esther display patience?

_____

_____

_____

_____

Why do you think Esther waited before she made her appeal, which does not come until Esther 7:1-6?

_____

_____

_____

_____

What new perspective does Esther's story give you on waiting on the Lord?

_____

_____

_____

_____

The Lord saved the Jews through Esther. And he saved David from destruction, as we saw in Psalm 40. But waiting on the Lord is not easy. The circumstances we are in when we're waiting on God can be hard to endure. The book of Lamentations gives us a picture of just how hard waiting can be. One of the saddest books of the Bible, it's a record of Jeremiah's grief—his prayers to God as he waits on God—in the wake of the Jewish exile to Babylonia. In the middle of the sorrow, however, comes a bright flash of hope. Read Lamentations 3:19-26. Write out the phrases or sentences in this passage which are especially meaningful for you. Add notes about why these words carry special meaning for you.

_____

_____

THE PATIENCE OF JESUS

During Jesus' time on earth, he—being the perfect image of God—provided us with even more evidence of God's patience. Many moments in the Gospel stories appear to be perfect times for Jesus to reveal himself as the Son of God and exert his authority. Instead, he waits. Jesus knew when it was the right time for something to happen, and when it was not yet the right time. He shows us that we can trust God as we wait on him with faith and patience, because we can trust God's wisdom and his timing absolutely. Waiting for God is a way in which we can be Christlike.

Read the following Gospel passages and write out the various ways in which Jesus waited:

Mark 1:32-34:

Mark 8:27-30:

Mark 9:2-10:

John 6:14-15:

Read John 12:23-33. What shift occurs in this passage?

_____

_____

_____

_____

From these Scriptures, what do you conclude about how Jesus saw the Father's plan for his life?

_____

_____

_____

_____

PATIENCE WITH EACH OTHER

In Jesus' parable, both servants fell to their knees and pleaded, "Be patient with me" (Matthew 18:26, 29). The Greek word here for "be patient" is *makrothumeo*. It is also translated "longsuffering." It literally means "to be long-tempered."

Being *long-tempered* is the opposite of being *short-tempered*. It involves self-restraint and the willingness to hold off from retaliation. It is what both servants in the parable begged their creditors to be. Don't clamp down on me yet, they said. Please suffer this situation a little longer. Be patient.

It's what God has been toward humanity since the beginning. And it's what he still is toward us today.

Read 1 Timothy 1:15-17. Why did Christ show "immense patience" to Paul?

_____

_____

_____

Write out 1 Timothy 1:16 with yourself in mind. You may even want to substitute your own name for "I" and "me."

_____

_____

_____

_____

As people who've been shown God's "long-temper," we, in turn, are called to be patient with each other.

For each of the following Scriptures, respond to the two questions listed in the two right columns:

	Written by	Addressed to	With whom are the letter's recipients called to be patient?	What other qualities accompany patience?
Ephesians 4:1-6	Paul	Believers in Ephesus, a pagan city (possibly to a wider audience)		
Colossians 3:12-14	Paul	Believers in Colossae who were exposed to false teachings about the nature of Christ		
1 Thessalonians 5:14-15	Paul	Believers in Thessalonica who had been converted from paganism		
2 Timothy 4:1-2	Paul, near the end of his life	Timothy, Paul's young fellow worker whom Paul calls "my true son in the faith" (1 Tim 1:2)		
James 5:7-11	James, brother of Jesus	Believers scattered due to persecution		

WAITING FOR CHRIST'S RETURN

Read Hebrews 6:10-12. The writer of Hebrews urges believers, "We do not want you to become lazy, but to imitate those who through faith and patience inherit what has been promised" (v. 12). If laziness means doing nothing, it would seem that laziness is patience! After all, lazy people are good at waiting.

Why do you think the writer of Hebrews draws a sharp contrast between being *lazy* and having *faith and patience?*

_____

_____

_____

_____

Read 2 Peter 3:1-15. Why do the scoffers express impatience with God (vv. 3-4)?

_____

_____

_____

_____

How does the Lord's view of time differ from ours (vv. 8-9)?

_____

_____

_____

_____

What reasons does Peter give for the Lord's patience with humanity (note especially vv. 9 and 15)?

_____

_____

_____

_____

What qualities should mark our lives as we wait patiently for the Lord's return (vv. 11, 14)?

_____

_____

_____

_____

In Samuel Beckett's play *Waiting for Godot*, the two characters Vladimir and Estragon spend the entire play waiting for someone named Godot, who never arrives. The two can't remember how long they've been waiting. And they don't know how long they will have to continue to wait.

Worse yet, Estragon and Vladimir can't remember why they are waiting for Godot. In fact, they're not even sure they know Godot or will recognize him if he does show up.

As they wait, the two learn through other characters who briefly appear that Godot is cruel, that he does not keep his promises and that he makes other people work for him while he does nothing. These unpleasant character traits are not enough to convince them to give up on Godot and leave, however. At the end of the play they are still waiting.

Are Vladimir and Estragon *patient*? It might seem that they are because they're willing to wait forever for the mysterious Godot. But a closer look shows us that their waiting is not, in fact, the kind of Christian patience we're studying, but rather *hopeless passivity*. They have no vibrant confidence in Godot; they have no eager anticipation of the good he will bring about in their lives. Their waiting is impersonal. They wait simply because waiting seems like their only choice. By contrast, to be patient in the biblical sense is to look to God with expectation even though we do not know what the fruit of our expectation will be. We wait for *him* because we trust him rather than circumstances or chance.

Shakespeare's Hamlet is another dramatic character who spends a good amount of time waiting. Hamlet's uncle Claudius has murdered Hamlet's father the king, assumed the throne of Denmark and married Hamlet's mother. The ghost of Hamlet's father appears and exhorts Hamlet to avenge his death, which Hamlet swears he will do.

So he waits . . . and waits. Opportunities do present themselves, but he doesn't follow through. Only when he knows he is dying, wounded by a poisoned rapier, does Hamlet finally take his vengeance out on the king.

Is Hamlet *patient?* It might seem that he is, because he withholds his hand and keeps putting off action. Hamlet himself gives a different interpretation of his lack of action, however. He berates himself for his spinelessness, calling himself "a rogue and peasant slave," "pigeon-livered," and various other insulting names in Elizabethan English whose force is now lost on us. He waits not for God's timing but for a burst of boldness sufficient to propel him into action. Hamlet's waiting, then, is not Christian patience but *cowardice*. Christian patience is *courageous*. To be patient in the biblical sense is not to shrink back but to remain bold as we wait for God's timing to go ahead and act.

Consider again the psalmists whose words you read in "Connect: Scripture to Scripture" (Psalm 5, 27, 33, 37, 38, 40, 130). Their writings show their steadfast hope in God and their courage in the face of unjust accusations and danger.

Consider Jeremiah standing in the ruins of Jerusalem. He lamented the city's destruction, yet he found the courage to express hope in God's faithfulness (Lamentations 3:19-26). His words in Lamentations have revived countless people's faith through the years, and continue to do so. If you have sung the hymn "Great Is Thy Faithfulness," for example, you've sung words inspired by Lamentations 3.

Consider Esther as well, who first waited and fasted for three days as she summoned courage to approach King Xerxes. She had her opportunity to plead for the lives of her people, but she put it off twice and waited until she sensed the time was right. Although the name of God is not mentioned in the book of Esther, the story strongly implies her confidence in God, which went along with her Jewish identity.

We've also seen how Jesus delayed the crisis point of his earthly life. When Jesus' time of revelation, suffering and death finally came, he met it with boldness because he knew it was his Father's perfect timing.

Although *Hamlet* and *Waiting for Godot* are great literature, they cannot provide models of Christian patience for us to emulate. Instead they show us cowardice and passivity. For examples of patience in the Christian sense, we can look to the psalmists, Jeremiah, Esther and of course the perfect example, Jesus Christ. These are the people who inspire us toward courage and expectation because, like them, we can trust God's work and God's timing.

What's the main idea in this section?

What is one thing you can act on based on this reading?

PART 4. DISCUSS
Putting It All Together

OPEN

What are your pet peeves? On a piece of paper finish the sentence "I hate it when people _____
_____." Put your papers in a bowl. Have each person draw one out and try to guess who wrote it.

READ MATTHEW 18:21-35.

Let's face it. Some people drive us up the wall. Annoying habits grate on our nerves until we begin practicing avoidance. With others we may try to pour out our love, but find them totally insensitive to us. We draw them out and ask questions, but they never show interest in learning about us.

1. What contrasts did you see in this passage when you studied it in part one?

2. Look back through the Old Testament examples of God's patience in "Connect: Scripture to Scripture." What clues do you get about the reasons for God's patience with humanity?

3. Consider the following statement: It would have been right for God *not* to be patient with humanity. Do you agree or disagree? Why?

4. How is Jesus Christ the perfect example of patience?

5. For whom (or for what) are you willing to wait a long time, and why?

6. The Greek word for "patience" in Matthew 18 literally means "long-tempered." In what situations are you most likely to be *short-tempered*, and why?

7. When and how has the Lord helped you to be long-tempered where you would naturally be short-tempered?

8. The servant in Jesus' parable was impatient with his fellow servant because he did not appreciate how much the king had forgiven him. Think of a person or group with whom you would like to "settle accounts" and exact what is due you (in any sense), as the servant did in verse 28. How does an appreciation of God's mercy affect the way you see that person or group?

9. When have you found that God's timing was far superior to your timing? To ask it another way, when have you been glad you waited for God?

10. The reading proposed that Christian patience is different from passivity and cowardice. In practical ways, how can you tell when you are exercising patience in the biblical sense and when you are only being passive or cowardly?

11. How do you react to the end of the parable (vv. 32-35) where it appears that the king's patience has run out?

12. So far as you know right now, what will be the biggest challenge to your patience this week?

Paul prayed that the Colossians would be "bearing fruit in every good work, growing in the knowledge of God, being strengthened with all power according to his glorious might so that [they might] have great endurance and patience, and giving joyful thanks to the Father, who has qualified [them] to share in the inheritance of the saints in the kingdom of light" (Colossians 1:10-12). Pray for those godly qualities for yourselves, focusing on great endurance and patience.

KINDNESS

2 Samuel 9

WHERE WE'RE GOING

Part 1. Investigate: 2 Samuel 9 (On Your Own)

Part 2. Connect: Scripture to Scripture (On Your Own)

Part 3. Reflect: A Note Under a Rock (On Your Own)

Part 4. Discuss: Putting It All Together (With a Group)

A PRAYER TO PRAY

Here's a prayer you can use to set you on your way:

Kind Father, you have shown us your heart through the kindness of your Son, and you continue your kindness daily through your Holy Spirit. You are merciful where you have every right to be harsh. You accept us when you have ample reason to reject us. May we be continually and increasingly amazed and grateful for your kindness to us and to all the world. Soften our hearts so that we will extend your kindness to those around us. Let others know that our kindness is not merely good nature or a pleasant personality but a supernatural quality which flows from your grace. Amen.

PART 1. INVESTIGATE
2 Samuel 9

Read 2 Samuel 9.

1. What characteristics of David stand out?

9:3. *A neck or spine injury could have made Mephibosheth a paraplegic, but it need not have been so extensive as that. Broken legs or ankles improperly set or poorly treated could likewise lame him. Splinting to set bones was a practice known in the ancient world, but compound fractures were often considered hopeless. [See 2 Samuel 4:1-4 for the explanation of Mephibosheth's injury.]*

2. What steps did David have to take to find Mephibosheth?

3. Put yourself in David's position. What reasons do you think David might have had for *not* being kind to Mephibosheth?

4. If David's kindness to Mephibosheth was not due to personal affection, what was it based on?

5. Think of a Mephibosheth in your own life (bear in mind that we are all handicapped in some way). As a Christian, what reasons do you have for showing kindness to that person?

9:4. *Lo Debar was an area north of the Yarmuk River in Transjordan that was allied with Saul and later transformed into a vassal state by David.*

6. In what specific ways did David show kindness to Mephibosheth?

7. In what practical ways can you show kindness to your Mephibosheth?

8. Look now at what happened from Mephibosheth's point of view. What thoughts or feelings do you think he had when summoned to appear before David?

9:7. Mephibosheth had good cause to be afraid of David. There is wide precedent in Mesopotamian texts for the elimination of all rival claimants to the throne when a king comes to power (compare Baasha's murder of Jeroboam's family in 1 Kings 15:29). Such purges also occurred years later as a form of revenge for political opposition or rebellion attempted against previous rulers. . . . David, however, treats Mephibosheth, the only surviving male member of the royal family, as the rightful heir to Saul's estates. His generosity is coupled with the command to eat at David's table.

9. What would he have felt as he heard the words recorded in verse 7?

10. What changes from his previous life would Mephibosheth now experience as someone who was "like one of the king's sons"? (Draw on your imagination as well as on what is in the passage.)

11. Think of people who have been especially kind to you. In what ways have you benefited from their kindness?

Spend some time thanking God for the people you thought of in question eleven—the people who have showed you kindness.

THOUGHTS FROM HAZEL

A knock came on our patio door. Outside was the mother of Ricky (not his real name), a ten-year-old boy whom our family knew, though not well. "Could I please talk to you for a little while?" she asked. I of course asked her to come in, and she tearfully told me the sad story of how Ricky had been born with some kind of disability that caused him a lot of difficulty in relating to other kids. I knew that kids made fun of Ricky. And I knew that he was never in our backyard with the rest of the neighborhood kids. But it had not registered with me how much he was being left out and made fun of.

My heart went out to him—and to his mother. I brought our two boys (then ten and eight) into the living room when Ricky's mom left. We had a talk about Ricky and about how much he needed love and a normal relationship with other kids in the neighborhood. I got some flak in the conversation ("He's no fun to play with." "He can't catch a ball." "He says weird things sometimes." "I'm afraid if we invite him over, the other kids won't want to play in our yard."). But then Mephibosheth came to mind. I had just written this study on kindness, and it occurred to me as we talked about Ricky that he must have felt incredibly left out too. I also remembered God's Spirit working in David's heart to show kindness to him. Now God was working in my heart to show kindness to Ricky.

It was the perfect opportunity to share the story with my young sons. By God's grace, I was able to help them see how *they* would feel if they were Ricky. And slowly, we all arrived at the same conclusion: Ricky would be invited to our yard and included totally in whatever was being played. I would call the other mothers and explain. Hopefully, working together, we could all help Ricky feel included.

It was a wonderful teaching opportunity for our boys. And Ricky was indeed included, and ended up fitting in better than they had feared.

Thank you, Holy Spirit of God, for your fruit of kindness.

PART 2. CONNECT
Scripture to Scripture

DAVID AND JONATHAN

King David extended kindness to Mephibosheth, as part one showed us. Who was this person Mephibosheth and why did King David seek him out? To find the answers we have to go into the book of 1 Samuel.

Samuel was a godly judge of Israel. (His sons, unfortunately, did not follow in his footsteps.) During his time of leadership, the people of Israel demanded that he appoint a king for them. Even after Samuel's warning that the king would not be good for the nation, the people insisted, "We want a king over us. Then we will be like all the other nations, with a king to lead us and to go out before us and fight our battles" (1 Samuel 8:19-20).

So Samuel obliged them. The appointed king, Saul, had many good qualities but also made many missteps so that eventually Samuel confronted him with the announcement that "now your kingdom will not endure; the LORD has sought out a man after his own heart and appointed him ruler of his people, because you have not kept the LORD's command" (1 Samuel 13:14).

The "man after God's own heart" was David. Samuel anointed him as king at the Lord's direction, but Saul remained in power. David became Saul's armor-bearer and musician, playing soothing harp music when Saul was tormented by an evil spirit, and he rose to a high rank in Saul's army. David also became fast friends with Saul's son Jonathan.

Terrified by David's ascending popularity and his ties with Jonathan, Saul repeatedly tried to kill David. But even Saul's animosity toward David could not kill the friendship between David and Jonathan.

Jonathan could not believe that his father wanted to kill David, but David understood Saul's heart better than Jonathan did. Read 1 Samuel 20:1-17 and paraphrase the answers to the following questions:

What did David ask Jonathan to do for him, and why (v. 8)?

_____

_____

_____

_____

What did Jonathan ask David to do for him, and why (vv. 14-15)?

_____

_____

_____

_____

The last time they saw each other, Jonathan said to David, "Go in peace, for we have sworn friendship with each other in the name of the LORD, saying, 'The LORD is witness between you and me, and between your descendants and my descendants forever'" (1 Samuel 20:42).

DAVID AND MEPHIBOSHETH

David was devastated when he heard the news that both Saul and Jonathan had been killed in a battle with the Philistines. Years later, he must have remembered Jonathan's entreaty to "show me unfailing kindness like the LORD's kindness as long as I live . . . and do not ever cut off your kindness from my family" (1 Samuel 20:14-15) because he went looking for someone remaining from the ravaged house of Saul "to whom I can show kindness for Jonathan's sake" (2 Samuel 9:1). His search ended with Jonathan's son Mephibosheth.

In 2 Samuel 9:1-7 David uses the word *kindness* three times. What is the reason for or source of each occurrence of *kindness*?

verse 1:

verse 3:

verse 7:

Some scholars question whether David's action toward Mephibosheth was purely out of good will or if it was a political move. Keeping Mephibosheth in Jerusalem and right at the king's table would keep him under close observation. He was, after all, "of the house of Saul," and therefore still suspect as an enemy of David. *The IVP Bible Background Commentary: Old Testament* notes, "Political prisoners were seldom kept in prison cells. It was more advantageous for the king to hold them in confinement within his palace or royal city, treating them to the pleasures of the 'king's table' but always keeping a close eye on their activities. Reports in ration lists from the Babylonian and Assyrian periods provide evidence of food, clothing and oil provided to 'guests' of the king. Persian courts contained political detainees as well as 'allies' who were kept in the king's presence to insure a continual flow of taxes and soldiers for the army. Thus Mephibosheth, like Jehoiachin many years later (2 Kings 25:27-30), enjoyed the largesse of the king's court but was not truly free."[1]

Even if David was holding Mephibosheth as a kind of political prisoner, however, Mephibosheth enjoyed kindnesses far beyond today's typical treatment of political prisoners and was clearly treated well.

Based on 2 Samuel 9, what do you think David's motives were in showing kindness to Mephibosheth?

_____

_____

_____

_____

THE KINDNESS OF GOD

In the English language, *kindness* is not a particularly strong word. When we think of *kindness,* we get a mild image of gentleness or thoughtfulness.

However, when David asked if there was still someone from Saul's household to whom he could show *kindness,* he meant something deeper than "I want to be nice to somebody." The Hebrew word used is *hesed,* often translated "loving-kindness" or "mercy," as we mentioned in session one. The force of the word is "the full flow of natural affection. . . . It is used of the goodness and abundant grace of God to his own people, his free favor and faithfulness; in man it is expressive of kindness and gratitude in a high degree, also of piety towards God; holiness, and zealous affection towards all that is good, and truly desirable."[2]

People may show *hesed* toward those in all stations of society: "toward family and relatives, but also to friends, guests, masters, and servants. *Hesed* toward the lowly and needy is often specified. The Bible prominently uses the term *hesed* to summarize and characterize a life of sanctification within, and in response to, the covenant. . . . Behind all these uses with man as subject, however, stand the repeated references to God's *hesed.* It is one of His most central characteristics. God's loving-kindness is offered to His people, who need redemption from sin, enemies, and troubles."[3]

The kindness of God is indeed a constant theme of Scripture. As Vine, Unger and White write, "The entire history of Yahweh's covenantal relationship with Israel can be summarized in terms of *hesed.* It is the one permanent element in the flux of covenantal history."[4]

God's *hesed* is especially prominent in the Psalms, where the word is often translated *steadfast love* or *mercy.* In Psalm 136, every verse includes the refrain "His love [kindness, loving-kindness] endures forever." The psalm reviews how God's kindness has been involved in every aspect of Israel's history.

Read Psalm 136 and, in the space below each category, write the numbers of the verses that refer to the various ways God has shown his kindness in that area.

Creation: _____

Israel's exodus from Egypt: _____

The conquest of Israel's enemies: _____

What words and phrases (besides the refrain) does the psalmist use to describe who God is?

_____

_____

_____

_____

KINDNESS IN THE OLD TESTAMENT

Joyce Baldwin writes, "Supremely [*hesed*] is the characteristic of God himself in his dealings with those who are his people. . . . People who have experienced the Lord's *hesed* are intended to reflect the same loving care in their relationships with others."[5] In other words, human kindness has the kindness of God as its source and can only flow from his kindness. Read the following Scriptures and identify for each passage whose kindness is meant, and what is expected from that kindness.

	Whose kindness is appealed to?	What kind act is requested?
Genesis 24:1-14		
Genesis 40:1-15		
Genesis 47:28-31		

Psalm 136 reviewed how God's *hesed* was involved throughout history. How do these three passages from Genesis fit into the Psalm 136 history of God's *hesed* for Israel?

_____

_____

_____

_____

Throughout Israel's history we find many examples of human kindness inspired by the kindness of the Lord. The kindness of Rahab in the book of Joshua is a beautiful illustration of this. As the Israelites under Joshua approached Canaan, Joshua sent two spies to scope out the land in general and the walled city of Jericho in particular. The spies hid in the house of Rahab, a prostitute. When the ruler of Jericho found out about them and demanded that Rahab give them up, she courageously protected them. She then asked for a return for her kindness.

Read Joshua 2:8-14. Paraphrase the dialogue in verses 12-14.

Rahab: "_____

_____."

The spies: "_____

_____."

Rahab seems an unlikely convert to Israel's God, but her words and her behavior show that her heart had been profoundly changed. Scholar Bruce Waltke explains, "After her confession of faith (9-11), the first in the Bible, Rahab sought salvation within the covenant community (12-13). In v. 12 kindness (Heb. *hesed*) is a shorthand way of saying 'unfailing help to a needy covenant partner.' God's salvation is available to all who seek him."[6] Those who, like Rahab, receive his extraordinarily kind gift of salvation are then empowered to show kindness to others.

Rahab is not the only Gentile woman in the Old Testament to be changed by the kindness of the God of Israel and show that kindness to others. In the time of the judges, the Moabite woman Ruth came to Bethlehem with her mother-in-law, Naomi. As Joyce Baldwin points out, "Ruth the Moabitess is said to have [shown loving care] (3:10) . . . because of her selfless loyalty to Naomi and because, by declaring Naomi's God to be her God, she entered into the sphere of his blessing. By the same route, other non-Israelites [like Rahab!] were able to know for themselves the Lord's *hesed,* for he is 'rich in love . . . he has compassion on all he has made' (Ps. 145:8-9)."[7] In Ruth and Naomi's story we find many examples of kindness wished for and expressed.

Read the book of Ruth, noting especially 1:8-9; 2:11-12, 19-20; 3:10-13; 4:13-17. Mark the following statements as true or false:

_____ Only Ruth and not Orpah showed kindness to Naomi.

_____ When Naomi heard that Ruth had gleaned in Boaz's field, Naomi praised Boaz's kindness.

_____ Boaz had heard of Ruth's kindnesses to Naomi.

_____ Naomi praised the Lord for his faithful kindness to their family.

_____ Ruth's kindness bore fruit in her life and in the lives of her descendants.

The story of Ruth shows that people do not need happy circumstances in order to demonstrate kindness. Unexpected kindness can arise in the most difficult situations. Even while Ruth was grieving the loss of her husband and then struggling to support the household once she and Naomi returned to Bethlehem, she maintained kindness to Naomi. This trait in her character did not go unnoticed by Boaz.

God's steadfast love did not change through the centuries of the Old Testament and, indeed, became more visible and knowable in Jesus Christ. Baldwin writes, "Supremely that steadfast love was revealed in Christ and is a secure basis for Christians' trust in the God of Naomi and Ruth today."[8]

THE LORD'S KINDNESS INCARNATE

In the New Testament, the fruit of the Spirit called *kindness* (Galatians 5:22) is the Greek word *chrestotes.* Just like *hesed* in the Old Testament, it is first of all a quality of God himself. Centuries after David showed the Lord's kindness to Mephibosheth, David's promised descendant, the Messiah, came to show the ultimate extent of the Lord's kindness to humanity.

Certainly Jesus Christ was a genuinely kind man. Peter described him as one who "went around doing good" (Acts 10:38). A simple reputation for good works, however, would not have gotten Jesus crucified. His kindness took radical risks. He was the God of *hesed* walking among people who spoke of God but did not care to live by *hesed.*

Read Titus 3:3-7. Paul succinctly describes our state before and after our rebirth in Christ. Verse 4 serves as the hinge between the two vivid descriptions. List Paul's descriptive phrases about us "before" and "after":

In our sinful state:

"But when the kindness and love of God our Savior appeared . . ."

In our reborn state:

Figure 5.1.

The letter to Titus is one of Paul's last known letters. It is doubtful that Titus or anyone Titus knew ever benefited directly from Jesus' good works of healing and teaching. The *kindness* of God from which they benefited was Jesus' payment for sin on the cross, by which they received "the washing of rebirth and renewal by the Holy Spirit" (Titus 3:5).

Read Ephesians 2:1-10. Write out verses 6-7, substituting your own name for the three occurrences of the word *us*.

_____

_____

_____

_____

What goes through your mind when you read that God will show the riches of his grace and his kindness to you "in the coming ages" too (v. 7)?

_____

_____

_____

_____

HOPE FOR ALL OF US

In the midst of Jesus' teaching about loving our enemies, there is a phrase which offers us immense hope. "Love your enemies, do good to them, and lend to them without expecting to get anything back. Then your reward will be great, and you will be children of the Most High, because he is kind to the ungrateful and wicked. Be merciful, just as your Father is merciful" (Luke 6:35-36).

When our hearts tell us that we are some of those "ungrateful and wicked," we can be reassured that God is kind to us. We have come to know and experience what Ephesians 2:7 calls "the incomparable riches of his grace, expressed in his kindness to us in Christ Jesus."

---

[1]John H. Walton, Victor H. Matthews and Mark W. Chavalas, *The IVP Bible Background Commentary: Old Testament* (Downers Grove, IL: InterVarsity Press, 2000), p. 336.

[2]William Wilson, "Kind, Kindness," in *Wilson's Old Testament Word Studies* (Peabody, MA: Hendrickson Publishers, 1900), p. 238.

[3]W. E. Vine, Merrill F. Unger and William White Jr., "Loving-Kindness," *Vine's Complete Expository Dictionary of Old and New Testament Words* (Nashville: Thomas Nelson Publishers, 1996), pp. 142-43.

[4]Ibid., p. 143.

[5]Joyce G. Baldwin, "Ruth," in *New Bible Commentary*, ed. G. J. Wenham, J. A. Motyer, D. A. Carson and R. T. France, 21st Century Edition (Downers Grove, IL: InterVarsity Press, 1994), p. 290.

[6]Bruce K. Waltke, "Joshua," in *New Bible Commentary*, ed. G. J. Wenham, J. A. Motyer, D. A. Carson and R. T. France, 21st Century Edition (Downers Grove, IL: InterVarsity Press, 1994), p. 240.

[7]Baldwin, "Ruth," p. 290.

[8]Ibid.

We have just learned about an upcoming documentary film titled *Kindness.* The moviemakers' aim is to celebrate acts of kindness in all forms, so the film will feature people recounting acts of kindness they have received or observed.

As we write this, volunteers are collecting interviews for the film. There is even a contest where people can submit their own kindness story via video, song, poem, animation or any other artistic form they choose, with a top prize of $1,000 going to the most compelling story.

Since the filmmakers never precisely define *kindness,* it's up to the story submitters to put their own meaning to the word. On the assumption that negative examples are also illuminating, the filmmakers will even accept stories of "no kindness."

We don't know how the *Kindness* filmmakers plan to verify people's stories. Perhaps we are cynical, but financial prizes must offer considerable enticement for people to exaggerate or even completely fabricate the stories of kindness they submit.

And, after all, the Internet is already full of dubious stories of kindness. The website www.snopes.com investigates and sometimes debunks urban legends, folklore and rumors. There is a special category, "glurge," for feel-good inspirational stories—the untraceable but supposedly true accounts of people (or sometimes animals) doing extraordinarily unselfish and heart-warming things. The details of when and where change with the retelling until there are multiple "true" versions. Even the plain impossibility of some stories does not stop people from passing them along. The popularity of glurge indicates how eager we are to believe that in spite of all the cruelty in the world, people can be—people *are*—kind to each other.

Perhaps even deeper than our desire to be-lieve people can be kind, though, is our desire to believe specifically that *strangers* can be kind. Strangers, after all, have no apparent reason to care. In Tennessee Williams's play *A Streetcar Named Desire,* Blanche DuBois is being led away to a mental institution when she directs her famous final line to the doctor: "Whoever you are, I have always depended on the kindness of strangers." Now, decades after Williams penned his script, the phrase "the kindness of strangers" is common parlance and has become the title of several books, songs, made-for-TV movies and a video-game feature. And stories of "the kindness of strangers" abound. Some, of course, are glurge; they sound too good to be true and in fact aren't true. Other stories of the kindness of strangers sound too good to be true but actually *are* true.

We experienced such kindness from strangers during a memorable summer when we traveled around and lived in a tent. Having recently decided to go into writing full time, we needed to find a less expensive and healthier place to live. So we put our furniture in storage, moved out of our apartment, and spent the summer working from the road and exploring small towns in northern Wisconsin and Minnesota.

In every town where we stayed, part of our exploration included visiting churches. We camped for over a week in one very small and picturesque town that held a lot of appeal. There were only two or three churches there, so we chose one to visit more or less at random. People asked us the usual questions: "Are you new in town?" "What brings you here?" (That week the town was having a reunion of *every* class that had ever graduated from the local high school, so we were also asked "What year did you graduate?")

When the people in that church learned

that we were living in a tent, however, they drew back. Their guard went up. We tried to be friendly and explained that we were only temporarily tenting while we explored their town as a place to live, but it didn't get us anywhere. Clearly we were not to be trusted. *Well, we thought, maybe they were just having a bad Sunday.* So the next Sunday we went back. One person greeted us with, "Are you still here?" Few others greeted us at all.

That evening, feeling discouraged, we left our campsite and went for ice cream. When we got back, something unusual was on the picnic table. It was a rock with a note under it. The message was simple: there's an apartment we might like to look at; it's not being advertised; it's a very nice apartment; here's the phone number. It was signed by a couple whose names we didn't recognize, with the added note that they were from the church we had visited. *That* church. The unfriendly one. Except here were two people who decided to be friendly, who bothered to drive to the campground and find out which site was ours and leave us a note, who chose to welcome us to their town. You don't tell people about apartments if you are hoping they'll move on.

The "glurge" version of our story would have us moving into that apartment, settling down in that town, becoming active members of that church and living there happily ever after. The truth is that the apartment was way above our price range, and the town was just too tiny for our tastes. We wound up buying our first house in a larger town a hundred miles away.

That was thirty years ago. We didn't keep the note and we don't remember the couple's names, but we've never forgotten what they did for us. Where other people were unfriendly, they were willing to be friendly. Where other people were unwelcoming, they were willing to extend a welcome.

A note under a rock on a picnic table isn't a big thing, unless it's exactly what the recipient needs right then. And while our story might not make it into the film *Kindness,* it has made it into this book. We are still grateful for the kindness of those strangers.

What's the main idea in this section?

What is one thing you can act on based on this reading?

PART 4. DISCUSS
Putting It All Together

OPEN

What are some reasons people have for being kind to others?

READ 2 SAMUEL 9.

The friendship between David and Jonathan, the son of David's mortal enemy, Saul, was powerful and loyal to the end. Just before they parted for the last time, David swore by his love to Jonathan that as long as both their houses existed, he would show kindness to Jonathan's descendants. This was a tremendous commitment because ordinarily when a king came to power, he banished all who had come before him. Many years later, David reigned over all of Israel. In 2 Samuel 9 his promise to Jonathan is fulfilled.

1. As a group, discuss your individual answers to question three from part one: Put yourself in David's position. What reasons do you think David might have had for *not* being kind to Mephibosheth?

2. How was the kindness of God revealed during Israel's history? Point out specific examples.

3. Rahab and Ruth, who both appear in the genealogy of Jesus, participated in the kindness of God. What did you learn in "Connect: Scripture to Scripture" about how these women experienced God's kindness and displayed God's kindness?

4. How did David and Jonathan defy Saul to express the kindness of God to one another?

5. What differences do you see between the kindness of Jesus Christ and "niceness"?

6. Describe your most profound experience(s) of God's kindness toward you.

7. How has God's kindness toward you helped you be more kind to other people?

8. Often television sitcoms focus on put-downs and sarcasm. Anything for a laugh! The message is that it isn't cool to be kind. How can the fruit of kindness poured through us make a difference in our cynical culture?

9. What typically keeps you from showing kindness to other people?

10. Think of a time when you saw or heard of someone extending kindness to an enemy (or a person connected with an enemy) as David extended kindness to Mephibosheth. What effect did it have on you?

11. Recall something kind that someone did for you this past week. What difference would it have made in your week if that person had not done that?

12. What is something kind that you could have done this week but didn't?

13. What is something kind that you can do for someone this week? Make specific plans to carry out that act of kindness.

Pray that others will see the kindness of God in and through you. Pray especially for friends who do not know Christ, that they will be attracted to him through your kindness.

SESSION SIX

GOODNESS

Psalm 107

WHERE WE'RE GOING

Part 1. Investigate: Psalm 107 (On Your Own)

Part 2. Connect: Scripture to Scripture (On Your Own)

Part 3. Reflect: There's No One Like Jesus (On Your Own)

Part 4. Discuss: Putting It All Together (With a Group)

A PRAYER TO PRAY

Here's a prayer you can use to set you on your way:

Lord God, everything that is good comes from you. You are all good-
ness. There is no evil or fault in you. We know that we are part of
your good creation, but we are fallen, corrupted by our rebellion
against you. Thank you for your mercy—for saving us, healing us,
leading us, blessing us. Thank you for welcoming us into the life of
your Son so that you see us in the light of his goodness. The world
worships so much that is ugly and depraved, the very opposite of
what is good; help us show them a different possibility. Help us to
reject the evil and choose the good in every decision we make, so that
the world sees your goodness in us. Amen.

PART 1. INVESTIGATE
Psalm 107

Read Psalm 107.

1. How do verses 1-3 introduce the major themes of the entire psalm?

2. The psalmist gives four illustrations of God's goodness in verses 4-9, 10-16, 17-22 and 23-32. What do each of these illustrations have in common?

3. What needs do the people have in each of these sections?

4. Which of these needs do you most relate to? (For example, we might experience the imprisonment of an addiction.)

5. Notice that in each situation the people call out to God for help. Is this usually your first reaction when you find yourself in distress? If not, what is?

107:10. *While most of those who had been deported to Babylon would not have been imprisoned, there would have been some political prisoners. Pits were used as prisons in most of the ancient Near East. The modern idea of a prison where prisoners were to be reformed into good citizens was foreign to the ancient world. Those in debt, criminals awaiting trial and political prisoners were held in confinement of one sort or another.*

107:16. *The Greek historian Herodotus described Babylon as having "one hundred gates in the circuit of the wall, all of bronze with bronze uprights and lintels." Large bronze gates have been excavated at the Assyrian period site of Balawat, giving a glimpse of what the Babylonian walls may have been like. Gates were locked by means of a bar slid across the gateway, and iron would obviously be the most difficult to break.*

107:29. *The sea was the most powerful image of uncontrolled chaos known to the ancient world. In the chaos combat motif featured in the mythologies as well as in the Old Testament, the* *forces of cosmic chaos were most frequently represented in the sea. Creation is sometimes spoken of as overcoming those forces and bringing order and control to the cosmos. In this context it is not the primordial past that is under discussion but Yahweh's ability to (again) bring the sea under control and restore order for these merchants. This idea of transforming cosmic acts into the historical realm occurs also in incidents like the Israelite crossing of the Red Sea, when the sea was harnessed and controlled by Yahweh to do his bidding. It should not be missed that this was a significant element in Jesus' calming of the sea as well.*

107:33-35. *In the world-upside-down motif, all that is considered most consistent and reliable is jeopardized. The concept can be applied to the cosmic realm (sun growing dark), the natural realm (mountains being leveled), the political realm (empires overthrown), the social realm (poor becoming rich) and the animal realm (lion and lamb together). It is often used in prophetic literature in connection with the Day of the Lord and coming judgment. The Babylonian epic of Irra is roughly similar in that it describes a reversal of Marduk's creation of order out of the original primeval chaos.*

6. Repeatedly the psalmist urges those who have been delivered to "give thanks to the Lord." Why do we need to be reminded of this?

7. According to the psalmist, what are some ways we should give thanks to God for his goodness and love (vv. 22, 32)?

8. What do verses 33-42 reveal about the ups and downs of life?

9. The psalmist concludes in verse 43: "Let the one who is wise heed these things." What things does he want us to heed?

10. How does seeing God answer the people's cry for help in this passage make the fruit of goodness more real to you?

11. In what ways can we imitate the goodness of God displayed in this psalm?

Spend some time praising God for his goodness. Name some specific examples of his goodness in your life and thank him for those glimpses of his character.

THOUGHTS FROM HAZEL

As I read the list of the fruit of God's Spirit, I asked myself, "Why did the apostle Paul include 'goodness' in his list? What does 'goodness' mean, really?" The first thing that came to mind was a giant bowl of tapioca pudding. That was *good*—but also bland. Not exactly an *exciting* dessert. Then I thought about how little kids are told to "be good." "Be good!" I would say to our boys when they were going to play at someone's house (along with "Be polite. Don't throw a baseball bat through a window. Be respectful to your friend's parents. Come home when you get bored so that you'll leave on a nice note."). Surely Paul had something more in mind than that when he included "goodness" in his list!

And then I ran across something that really helped me. I was reading J. I. Packer's *Knowing God* for the second time, and among the many helpful things he says, I read in these words in chapter sixteen (titled "Goodness and Severity"):

> The classical exposition of God's goodness is Psalm 107. Here, to enforce his summons to "give thanks to the Lord, for he is good," the psalmist generalizes from past experiences of Israel in captivity and Israelites in personal need to give four examples of how people "cried out to the Lord in their trouble, and he delivered them from their distress" (vv. 1, 6, 13, 19, 28): First, God's redeeming the helpless from their enemies; second, delivering from "darkness and the shadow of death" the ones he had himself brought into this condition because of their rebellion against him; third, healing the diseases with which he had chastened the "fools" who disregarded him; and fourth, protecting voyagers by stilling the storm which they thought would sink their ship. Each episode ends with the refrain, "'Let them give thanks to the Lord for his unfailing love and his wonderful deeds for men.'" The whole psalm is a majestic panorama of the operations of divine goodness, transforming human lives.[1]

Seeing God answer people's cry for help in this passage made the fruit of goodness more real to me. It caused me to want to imitate God in ministering to helpless people I know, to find creative ways to let unbelievers in on the wonder of what Jesus has done for them, to really minister to those who are sick, and, in some way, to help people with various "storms" in their lives really partake of God's goodness.

---

[1] J. I. Packer, *Knowing God*, 20th Anniversary ed. (Downers Grove, IL: InterVarsity Press, 1993), p. 163.

Part 2. Connect
Scripture to Scripture

REVOLUTIONARY GOODNESS

For thousands of years philosophers have debated the concept of goodness, coming up with all kinds of ideas about what goodness is and how to define it. Scripture offers a different perspective on goodness. In Scripture, goodness is not a *what* but a *who*. It is not an abstract concept; it is personal.

Goodness resides in the character of God. The only reason human beings know anything about goodness is because the One who created us is good.

The idea that God is good was an unorthodox idea in the pagan nations surrounding Israel and later in the context of the Roman and Greek gods surrounding the early Christians. Unlike the one true God, pagan gods were seen as temperamental, demanding and indifferent to human feelings. J. I. Packer draws this contrast: "In place of a cluster of gods who are all too obviously made in the image of man, and who behave like a crowd of Hollywood film stars, the Bible sets the one almighty Creator, the only real God, in whom all goodness and truth find their source, and to whom all moral evil is abhorrent."[1]

With J. I. Packer's words in mind, read Psalm 107:1 and then write it out word-for-word:

_____

_____

_____

_____

We are commanded to give thanks to the Lord. Why? *Because he is good.* When the psalmist adds that God's love endures forever, the implication is that the enduring nature of God's love comes from his goodness.

The goodness of God is not something that comes and goes according to his moods. "Goodness," scholars explain, "is in accordance with God's nature. As it is in the nature of water to be wet or fire to be hot, it is the nature of God to be good. This characteristic is not changeable or diminishing, nor does it have a beginning or an end."[2]

Psalm 107 goes on to describe various bad situations of distress, hunger, danger, lostness, imprisonment, rebellion and other crises. In all these circumstances the sufferers cried out to God, and he rescued them. They are urged to give thanks. The psalmist's big reason for giving thanks, however, is not in the specifics of anyone's deliverance. The big reason is that *God is good.*

Think about the fact that the goodness of God outweighs even the specific blessings he has given you, as good as they are. When have you been especially aware that God's goodness is even better than his good gifts?

_____

_____

_____

_____

A GOOD CREATOR, A GOOD CREATION

Only a good God could create a good world, and that is what God did. The author of Genesis tells us, "God saw all that he had made, and it was very good" (1:31). A bad god would create a bad world—and while many aspects of our world look bad here and now in the wake of the Fall, the goodness of God's creation—the goodness of his design and his intentions for the world—still shows through.

God's declaration in Genesis 1:31 that everything he'd made was "very good" was not the first time he deemed something on earth *good*. At each intermediate step in his creation process he made a similar acknowledgment.

Read Genesis 1, considering each good step of creation. What does each of the following parts of creation communicate to you about the goodness of God?

light (vv. 3-5):

sky, water and dry ground (vv. 6-10):

vegetation (vv. 11-13):

sun, moon and stars (vv. 14-19):

fish and birds (vv. 20-23):

land animals (vv. 24-25):

human beings (vv. 26-31):

KNOWING GOOD AND EVIL

Read Genesis 2:6-25. The first man and woman were free to enjoy the fruit from all the trees in Eden—except one. That tree has an interesting name: the tree of *the knowledge of good and evil*. In your own words, explain what you think *the knowledge of good and evil* means.

_____

_____

_____

_____

At this point Adam and Eve had an intimate relationship with God, who is all good. We presume they had no experience of evil. What do you think the words *good* and *evil* meant to them?

_____

_____

_____

_____

Read Genesis 3:1-6. We don't know how long the first humans resisted sampling the forbidden fruit. They gave in after Satan told Eve, among other things, "God knows that when you eat from it your eyes will be opened, and you will be like God, knowing good and evil" (Genesis 3:5).

Why do you think Eve was attracted by the possibility of knowing good and evil?

_____

_____

_____

_____

Read Genesis 3:7-13, 21-24. In what senses had Adam and Eve come to understand the difference between good and evil?

_____

_____

_____

_____

EXPERIENCING GOD'S GOODNESS

Even in their sinful and fallen state, the human race remained aware of the goodness of God. The writers of the Psalms were nearly obsessed with God's goodness and how his goodness was manifest in their experience.

You have already read about the goodness of God in Psalm 107. The following excerpts from other psalms also speak of God's goodness. Match up each reference with the specific aspect of God's goodness that each psalmist experienced.

Psalm 23	God's forgiveness
Psalm 31:19-20	God's closeness
Psalm 34:8-10	God's compassion
Psalm 73:23-28	God's commandments
Psalm 86:5-7	God's mighty acts
Psalm 100:4-5	God's provision
Psalm 119:65-68	God's mercy
Psalm 145:3-7	God's protection
Psalm 145:8-9	God's faithfulness

A PICTURE OF GOODNESS

In about 587 B.C. the Babylonian army under Nebuchadnezzar was besieging Jerusalem. The prophet Jeremiah discerned that the attack was in the purposes of God, and that the Jews would be exiled to Babylon because of their persistent idolatry. Jeremiah proclaimed this publicly and advised the people to surrender, which, naturally, didn't make him very popular with the king and other officials. Jeremiah was "confined in the courtyard of the guard in the royal palace of Judah" (Jeremiah 32:2). His imprisonment could not stop the Spirit of the Lord from speaking to him, though, and he continued to receive "the word of the Lord."

In the midst of warnings of judgment, God gave Jeremiah messages of hope. The exile to Babylon would not be the end of the story. Read Jeremiah 32:36-44. Write out what God says to the people of Judah in verses 40-41.

_____

_____

_____

_____

Based on this passage, draw images of what that promised "good" will look like. Include words or images for what that promised "good" might sound like, smell like, taste like, feel like as well.

God kept talking to Jeremiah about the goodness of the coming restoration. Read Jeremiah 33:1-13. (Verse 11 is a quote from Psalm 107:1 and other psalms.)

Identify the activities which are going on in this restored land and why each of them could be called "good."

Activity	Why it is "good"

As the *Dictionary of Biblical Imagery* notes, "This is indeed the proverbial good life, with God and people in harmony and people rejoicing in both God and the human blessings that he bestows. The goodness of God is not isolated from life but is the basis for what is good in it."[3]

HE HAS SHOWED YOU WHAT IS GOOD

In addition to demonstrating his goodness throughout history, God also explicitly stated, through the prophet Micah, how we are to live out the goodness he has showered on us. Read Micah 6:6-8. Give a real-life example of someone doing each of the good things mentioned in verse 8.

_____

_____

_____

_____

THE RIGHTEOUS BRANCH

Read Jeremiah 33:14-18. Here God declares through Jeremiah that the days are coming "when I will fulfill the good promise I made to the people of Israel and Judah" (Jeremiah 33:14). What will the promised righteous Branch accomplish?

_____

_____

_____

_____

The Branch was also prophesied by Isaiah (Isaiah 11:1-5). Christians understand this Branch to be Jesus Christ.

Jesus' message from the beginning was called "the good news" (Mark 1:1, 15). Speaking to an assembly of Gentiles, the apostle Peter said they knew "how God anointed Jesus of Nazareth with the Holy Spirit and power, and how he went around doing good and healing all who were under the power of the devil, because God was with him" (Acts 10:38).

Jesus proclaimed good news and he did good. Yet when a man addressed him as "Good teacher" and asked how to inherit eternal life, Jesus gave a surprising answer. Read Mark 10:17-18. Write out Jesus' response in verse 18.

_____

_____

_____

_____

According to Jesus, if we call him "good," what are we saying?

_____

_____

_____

_____

In Jesus' own day, people were divided about who he really was. Some believed his claims to be God while others dismissed him as crazy. Irrespective of opinions, though, in Jesus there resided a quality of goodness which no human being could match. Even today, when Christianity is often publicly sneered at, it is *Christians* who are the target rather than Jesus himself. People who don't like Christianity can find plenty of negative things to say about Christians, but they have trouble finding anything negative to say about the goodness of Jesus; his life silences his critics. He is just too manifestly good.

GOD THE SOURCE OF ALL GOODNESS

When life gets hard, people who are trying to trust and serve the Lord can have doubts about his goodness, particularly when life gets hard *because* of their faith. Suffering leads many to doubt God's goodness and therefore to withdraw their trust in him. Reconciling God's goodness and the evil in the world is beyond the scope of this study, but we come closest to an answer when we look at the incarnation. Tim Keller writes that in Jesus Christ, God became fully human and experienced every evil that human beings can experience:

> On the cross [Jesus] went beyond even the worst human suffering and experienced cosmic rejection and pain that exceeds ours as infinitely as his knowledge and power exceeds ours. In his death, God suffers in love, identifying with the abandoned and god-forsaken. Why did he do it? The Bible says that Jesus came on a rescue mission for creation. He had to pay for our sins so that someday he can end evil and suffering without ending us.[4]

James wrote his letter to persecuted Christians who were having doubts about the goodness of God. Read James 1. Write out verse 17. If you're able, write it out in several different translations (see www.biblestudytools.com/compare-translations).

On a separate piece of paper, list as many of those "good and perfect gifts" as you can. Include not only material things but spiritual blessings, relationships, happenings in your life, reassurances and emotional blessings. Keep the list and keep adding to it daily for a week. Use your list to prompt you to continually thank God for his goodness.

---

[1]J. I. Packer, *Knowing God*, 20th Anniversary ed. (Downers Grove, IL: InterVarsity Press, 1993), p. 180.

[2]Leland Ryken, James C. Wilhoit and Tremper Longman III, gen. eds., "Goodness," in *Dictionary of Biblical Imagery* (Downers Grove, IL: InterVarsity Press, 1998), p. 344.

[3]Ibid.

[4]Timothy Keller, *The Reason for God: Belief in an Age of Skepticism* (New York: Riverhead Books, 2008), p. 30.

PART 3. REFLECT
There's No One Like Jesus

We lived near a large city and usually caught the local news at 6:00 p.m. It was depressing. More than that, it was alarming—nothing but bad news. The lead story was always some local disaster. And the more heartrendingly tragic the event was, the more air time it received. The impression given was that nothing good ever happened in that city.

When the national news came on, it wasn't any better. Now we don't have a television, but the news on the Internet is no improvement. Bad news still dominates the headlines.

Does bad news get more coverage because only bad things happen in the world? Hardly. The producers of news have an obvious attention-getting strategy. Bad news grabs people's eyes and ears. It seizes people's emotions and keeps viewers watching. Broadcasters are afraid that more cheerful fare will mean boredom and a lost audience.

Perhaps they're wrong, though. Enough viewers must have complained about the bad news monopoly, because news broadcasts have started to include segments on people doing positive things. Good news is finding some broadcast room, although it is usually relegated to a special feature toward the end of the program.

Jesus lived in a fallen world surrounded by bad news. As the only sinless person who ever lived, he must have been acutely sensitive to evil. Yet he never gave in to the wash of negativity around him. He kept announcing good news. He also kept demonstrating goodness in his life. He consistently "went around doing good" (Acts 9:38).

One of the most rewarding aspects of working on our book *Living Your Legacy* was the opportunity to dig up stories of good things people are doing. Our focus was specifically on actions by older adults, but the pleasure

that comes from hearing the stories has no age limit. The efforts we uncovered have not made headlines, but they have made a tremendous difference to many people.

For example, one Christian woman saw a need in her small town and went into action to do something about it. When the only coffee shop in town closed, she thought the town's residents still needed a place to get together in the early morning and talk. She therefore persuaded a church to open their doors at 6:00 a.m. every weekday morning for people to come in and have a morning cup of coffee for free. Arriving early to get the coffee going, she doesn't have to wait long for townspeople to show up; people sit around tables and chat about the news or books they're reading and generally catch up on each other's lives while low-key Christian music plays in the background. And if someone is missing, they take note.

Filling a gap by creating a friendly gathering place is a good thing!

Another instance of goodness occurred recently in a very small town near us. When heavy rains and flooding just about wiped out the town, volunteers provided immediate relief and then went on to form a nonprofit organization to help with ongoing recovery. At Christmas, three months after the disaster, volunteers welcomed flood-victim families to an American Legion Hall for a Christmas celebration. The families enjoyed a turkey dinner, a visit from Santa Claus and gifts for all the children.

Bringing comfort to traumatized families is a good thing!

In a similar example, a church in our city provides free food to people three times a week. It's not a government program or even a program with income limits. It's a ministry of reclaiming perfectly good food that would otherwise be thrown out by restaurants, grocery stores, bakeries, hospital food services and other places that routinely prepare excess food. Everything is meticulously organized, and the atmosphere is cheerful and upbeat, turning what could be demeaning into a positive social event.

Providing food for people in need and refusing to waste food are good things![1]

While contemporary culture may mock the idea of *goodness,* everyone would recognize the above efforts and others like them as *good.* There is also a person whom everyone acknowledges as good, and that is Jesus Christ.

Nobody accuses Jesus himself of any evil. As we mentioned in part two, people may find fault with Christians but they don't generally find fault with Christ. Critics of Christianity do not accuse Christians of being *too much* like Jesus, but of being *not enough* like Jesus.

Even if skeptics deny that Jesus is the Son of God or the Savior of the world, even if they deny that he rose from the dead, even if they insist that he was only a man, they acknowledge that he was a good man. And even people we would label "bad"—as well as people who would label themselves "bad"—recognize that *Jesus is good.* Three times Pilate said, "I find no basis for a charge against him" (John 18:38; 19:4, 6). The Roman centurion in charge of crucifying him said, "Surely this man was the Son of God!" (Mark 15:39). Who else could earn such high regard from those who would be expected to despise him?

The news may depress us and high-profile Christians may embarrass us when they fall, but we can always trust in the goodness of Jesus. And we can trust him to empower us through his Spirit to be people who are good and who do good things, in the midst of an evil and broken world. *He is good.*

What's the main idea in this section?

What is one thing you can act on based on this reading?

---

[1]Stories taken from Dale and Sandy Larsen, *Living Your Legacy: An Action-Packed Guide for the Later Years* (Downers Grove, IL: InterVarsity Press, 2012), pp. 39, 70-71, 108.

PART 4. DISCUSS
Putting It All Together

OPEN

Do you consider yourself to be a pretty good person? Explain.

READ PSALM 107.

Psalm 107 is the classic exposition of God's goodness. God's actions reveal goodness in its highest and purest form. His goodness provides the standard for developing this fruit in our own lives.

1. As a group, discuss your individual answers to question one from part one: How do verses 1-3 introduce the major themes of the entire psalm?

2. What did you learn in "Connect: Scripture to Scripture" about the various ways we can experience God's goodness?

3. Adam and Eve ate from the forbidden tree of the knowledge of good and evil. Why would it have been better for humanity to *not* know the difference between good and evil?

4. Look back at your answers to question two from part one: The psalmist gives four illustrations of God's goodness in different times of need in verses 4-9, 10-16, 17-22 and 23-32. Share with the group which of these needs you most relate to.

5. When and where are you most aware of the goodness of God, and why?

6. When and where are you most prone to forget or question the goodness of God, and why?

7. People often accuse Christians of being hypocrites who pretend to be good but aren't. What do you think is the best way to counter these charges of hypocrisy?

8. Think of a time when you discovered that you were not as good as you thought. What did you do when you came to that realization?

9. What specific disciplines and habits have helped you to put goodness into practice in concrete ways? Think about good things you try to do regularly whether you feel like it or not.

10. The psalmist offers some ways we should give thanks to God for his goodness (vv. 2, 22, 32). How can you take the psalmist's advice and do those things this week?

Pray that you will see the goodness of God all around you. Thank God for his forgiveness in Christ, and pray that others will see God's goodness in and through you.

FAITHFULNESS

2 Chronicles 20:1-30

WHERE WE'RE GOING

Part 1. Investigate: 2 Chronicles 20:1-30 (On Your Own)

Part 2. Connect: Scripture to Scripture (On Your Own)

Part 3. Reflect: A Faithful Teacher (On Your Own)

Part 4. Discuss: Putting It All Together (With a Group)

A PRAYER TO PRAY

Here's a prayer you can use to set you on your way:

God of all faithfulness, you remain steadfast when the world all around us is changing and when our own hearts are fickle and fearful. Our love for you is intermittent while your love for us is constant. Put our feet on solid ground. Help us to know and believe how reliable you are, so that we will become reliable ourselves. Let us be people others can count on. We ask this in the name of Jesus Christ who is the same yesterday, today and forever. Amen.

PART 1. INVESTIGATE
2 Chronicles 20:1-30

20:31. *According to Thiele, Jehoshaphat ruled 872-848 B.C., and most other reckonings only differ a year or two from those dates. It has been suggested that he was coregent with his father Asa for the first three years of his reign. Contemporary kings in Israel were Ahab, Ahaziah and Joram. Ashurnasirpal II and Shalmaneser III ruled Assyria. No references to Jehoshaphat have yet been found in extrabiblical materials.*

20:2. *The location of Hazazon Tamar is unknown, but some have placed it near the southern end of the Dead Sea, possibly at el-Hasasa, between En Gedi and Bethlehem. The oasis of En Gedi lies midway down the Dead Sea and approximately thirty-five miles southeast of Jerusalem. Fed by a continuous spring, it is a splash of life and color in the midst of an otherwise barren landscape. It has served as a cultic site, military outpost and commercial center during its long history. There are a number of fortresses from the period of the monarchy that have been discovered in this area. One is at the spring, while another is at the top of the cliff that offers a view of travelers for miles around.*

Jehoshaphat, king of Judah, learned about faithfulness the hard way. He began his reign by faithfully obeying God's commands (2 Chronicles 17:3-9). But he entered into a military alliance with Ahab, king of Israel, against God's will. The results were disastrous and God was displeased. No wonder Jehoshaphat was anxious when invading armies approached his kingdom! In his desperation he cried out to God. God's answer, recorded in this passage, is an amazing illustration of faithfulness.

Read 2 Chronicles 20:1-30.

1. Use your imagination to fill in the details of the passage. Now describe what you see (the setting, the mood, the people and so on) in verses 1-13.

   in verses 14-19.

   in verses 20-30.

2. Now imagine yourself specifically as one of the Israelites in verses 3-4. What are you feeling?

3. Examine Jehoshaphat's prayer (vv. 6-12). On what basis does he appeal to God for help?

4. How would Jehoshaphat's view of God encourage him and the people to trust God in this crisis?

5. Now consider God's response to Jehoshaphat's prayer (vv. 14-17). How would the prophet's words have required faith from the people?

6. What evidence is there that the people believed his message (vv. 18-21)?

7. Have you ever praised God in the middle of a problem—before an answer came? Explain why or why not.

8. How would you have felt as you "came to the place that overlooks the desert and looked toward the vast army" (v. 24)?

9. Describe the effects God's faithfulness had on the people (vv. 25-30).

10. What can we learn about faithfulness from the example of Jehoshaphat and the people of Judah in this passage?

11. How can an awareness of God's faithfulness to us impact the way we treat others?

20:19. *The Kohathites and the Korahites were two of the principle families that were involved in the leadership of the Jerusalem temple during the period of the monarchy. They were also two of the most important Levitical families (or clans). In the genealogy of 1 Chronicles 6:22–24 (also see Ex 6:18; 1 Chron 6:31), the Korahites were descended from the Kohathites.*

20:28. *The lyre had a widespread use in the ancient Near East. Egyptian tomb paintings show individuals from the Transjordan playing the lyre. The harp was evidently used in Nebuchadnezzar's orchestra (see Dan 3). In Israel it was a wooden instrument with eight strings (see 1 Chron 15:21). There were different types of trumpets used in ancient Israel. This particular type of trumpet was used on military and religious occasions to summon the people. Trumpets are occasionally depicted in the art of the ancient Near East, including the bronze figure of a trumpet player from Caria in southwest Turkey (c. 800 B.C.).*

Spend time thanking God for his faithfulness to you in the past. Praise him for his present involvement in your life. Ask him to help you grow in faithfulness to him and others.

THOUGHTS FROM HAZEL

I had just sent the last study of this guide to InterVarsity Press several years ago, and I was looking forward to tackling some other projects that had piled up when our youngest son, Randy, burst into the house and said, "I'm feeling really awful!" He hadn't been feeling well for several days, but in that moment, as he sat down in a chair, he howled with pain. We didn't know it right then, but his appendix had burst. Dave got him into the car and took off for the hospital while I called the emergency room to ask them to have a gurney waiting when they got there. Then I called our next-door neighbors to see if they could take *me* to the hospital.

When I arrived, Randy was in the trauma section of the ER, throwing up and crying out in pain. I told the doctor he had been sick for five days, but the doctor seemed oblivious. "I'll do a CAT scan," he said, "but not for a while. He can't keep the liquid down until he stops vomiting." Then he went back out to his station, where I saw him laughing and talking with his cohorts.

Meanwhile, Randy got sicker and sicker. I could hear my boy screaming with pain through the door of the ER. And I grew frantic. Rushing over to the doctor I said, "You've *got* to give him the CAT scan! He's going to die!" Nonchalantly the doctor went into the room where Randy and Dave were and finally consented to a CAT scan. Afterward, he came out and reported that Randy's appendix had burst and surgery was needed. "Can we get the show on the road *right now*?" I asked. He agreed and left to call the surgeon. By that time, it was 2:00 in the morning.

The surgeon came. Randy was prepped and operated on. Dave stayed the night while I went home to try to get a few hours of sleep.

The next morning, I saw my boy in his (private) hospital room with a private nurse. The surgeon came in and checked on Randy. Then he said to me, "This is one lucky guy. He came as close to death as it's possible to get."

I thought of Jehoshaphat and the fruit of faithfulness. And I thought of Jehoshaphat's wonderful prayer in 2 Chronicles 20:6, 7 and 12: "Are you not? Did you not? Will you not?" God's answer, in effect, was, "Go out to battle with men you have appointed to praise me for the splendor of my holiness!" I began to draw on the fruit of faithfulness and to praise God for saving Randy's life.

It was three weeks before Randy was well enough to be moved from the hospital to our local aftercare facility. His whole system had been so filled with bacteria that it took five weeks to get it all straightened out. He was hardly able to eat anything during those five weeks and was like a wraith when he came home. But, because of the fruit of faithfulness, my heart was calm.

PART 2. CONNECT
Scripture to Scripture

Scripture overflows with images of God keeping his promises. Indeed, God's faithfulness is a constant theme in Scripture, and the faithful God himself is a constant presence to his people in Scripture.

A PROMISE OF OFFSPRING AND LAND

We don't have to look very far in the Bible to find God making promises. Genesis is full of examples. One of the most well known, perhaps, is the story of God's promises to Abraham and Sarah. The couple longed for a child, but at their advanced age it seemed impossible. God had already promised to make a great nation from Abraham's offspring, but not even one child was forthcoming. When Abraham complained to God about the situation, God intensified his promise. In the following Scriptures, what was promised, and to whom?

	What did God promise?	To whom did God promise it?
Genesis 15:1-5		
Genesis 15:17-19		
Genesis 17:1-7		
Genesis 17:15-16		
Genesis 17:19-21		
Genesis 18:10-14		

The fulfillment of God's promise to give Abraham and Sarah a son comes in Genesis 21:1. Write out the verse word for word:

_____

_____

_____

_____

Scripture also shows us what happened regarding God's promises about land—the Promised Land, as it's often called. It's easy for us to use that title for the land (Canaan) that God gave to Abraham's descendants and not think about the grammar of the phrase. It is the *Promised Land*; it is a *land* which was *promised*.

Moses led the Israelites out of Egypt, but it was Joshua who led them into the Promised Land. At the end of his life, Joshua addressed the people and reviewed what had happened under his leadership. Read Joshua 23:1-5. How was God faithfully keeping his promise to bring the Israelites into their Promised Land?

_____

_____

_____

_____

DAVID AND BEYOND

Another well-known Old Testament figure God made promises to, in addition to Abraham, was David. Psalm 89 gives us a good picture of God's promises—and faithfulness—to David and his descendants. Read the psalm and write the numbers of all the verses that refer to the Lord's faithfulness.

_____

_____

_____

_____

The psalm makes an abrupt shift of mood at verse 38. How would you explain the contrast in tone between verses 1-37 and verses 38-51?

_____

_____

_____

_____

Scholars are unsure who the author of this psalm is and when it was written. There are two "Ethans" we know of who lived during the time of David and Solomon. It's possible that one of them wrote the first thirty-seven verses and that someone else wrote verses 38 through 51 several hundred years later (perhaps during the exile to Babylon). Or it could be that the whole thing was written hundreds of years after David, and that the reference to Ethan the Ezrahite at the beginning of the psalm simply indicates what type of psalm it is—one that's in the tradition of psalms by Ethan. In any case, the psalmist is very aware of the promises God made to David and of his faithfulness thus far.

Complete this sentence:

Despite the change of mood, the last part of this psalm (vv. 38-51) still expresses confidence in God's faithfulness because

_____

_____

The psalmist could not have imagined the far-reaching impact of God's promises to David. Today we understand that these promises of faithfulness to David—promises that stretch back into Genesis and forward into the New Testament on up to today and into the future—are fulfilled in Jesus Christ.

Read the mysterious promise God made in Genesis 3:14-15, just after Adam and Eve sinned in the Garden. In your own words, describe what would transpire between the serpent and the offspring of the woman.

_____

_____

_____

_____

_____

Now read Matthew 1 and Luke 1:26-38.

In light of Psalm 89 and Genesis 3, where do you see God's faithfulness in these passages?

_____

_____

_____

_____

_____

Fill in the blanks for Luke 1:31-33: "You will be with child and _____ to a son, and you are to give him the name _____. He will be _____ and will be called the _____. The Lord God will give him the _____ of his father _____, and he will _____ over the house of Jacob _____; his kingdom will _____."

What new promises do the angel's words to Mary introduce?

_____

_____

_____

_____

_____

Jesus' birth was a partial fulfillment of God's promises; his death and resurrection, of course, are also hugely important pieces of the fulfillment of God's promises.

Read John 19:28-30; 20:1-18, part of John's account of Jesus' death and resurrection.

Fill in the chart below by listing any details that you think are examples of faithfulness, and then answering why you think each detail is a good example of faithfulness.

Examples of Faithfulness	Why It's an Example of Faithfulness

Christ is the ultimate proof of God's faithfulness. God did not abandon humanity to the destruction of sin. God sent a Savior who did not waver in his purposes but who remained steadfast to the completion of his mission.

CHRIST IS FAITHFUL

Though Scripture continually points forward to Jesus, the Messiah, and despite Jesus' resurrection, some of the Jews still clung to Old Testament habits and perspectives, including the greatness of Moses. When Moses was leading the Israelites through the desert, after all, God spoke approvingly of him, that "he is faithful in all my house" (Numbers 12:7). Yet Moses was fallible. His failings denied him entrance into Canaan. Other leaders and prophets all had their flaws as well. Only Jesus Christ was—and is—completely reliable.

Read Hebrews 3:1-6. Note the ways in which Jesus and Moses are similar and different:

How Jesus and Moses Are Similar	How Jesus and Moses Are Different

We need others to help us on our journey, but placing all of our trust in anyone but Jesus is setting ourselves up for disappointment, or even worse. He alone will never deceive us, manipulate us, betray us or disappoint us. He alone is completely faithful.

In his first letter to the Corinthian church, Paul made several powerful statements that help us grasp even more the faithfulness of God. Read 1 Corinthians 1:1-9. Write out verses 8 and 9 word for word:

_____

_____

_____

_____

_____

_____

Now read 1 Corinthians 10:1-13.

This passage warns against _____.

It assures us that God is _____.

It promises that God will _____.

In the space below, write out the dates of significant events in your life. If you don't remember a precise date, write a phrase about the event ("trip to Mexico," "Lara's car accident"). Dates stick in our memories because of both joy and sorrow, so include dates which mark both happiness and sadness. Include future dates you are anticipating (a birth, a graduation, a move to a new home). If today is especially significant for you, include today's date.

_____

_____

_____

_____

_____

_____

_____

Now read Hebrews 13:8. Circle all the dates above on which Jesus Christ was, is or will be the same as he has always been.

PART 3. REFLECT
A Faithful Teacher

Two china teacups and saucers sat on a bookshelf in our living room. One cup was delicate, nearly translucent, deep blue with swirls of green. The cup was not nestled securely in the saucer but stood on three small china feet. The other teacup was ordinary, cream-colored, rather plain with only a bit of gold decoration.

One day a family was visiting and the kids were playing near the bookcase.

CRASH!

Silence.

The delicate blue cup and saucer lay smashed on the floor. Sandy took one look at the splinters of broken china and said, "Hooray!"

She didn't care about the blue cup. It was something she had gotten in a rummage sale for fifty cents. The other teacup—the plain cream-colored one which was still safe on the shelf—was a present from her second-grade teacher when she graduated from high school.

Of course, Sandy received a number of high-school graduation presents. Most of them have been lost or discarded over the years. Why does she still cherish this gift from Florence Ward, her second-grade teacher?

For starters, Miss Ward was the first adult (other than Sandy's parents) who encouraged her to write. Sandy hated school until the day Miss Ward had the class cut out magazine pictures, paste them at the top of a piece of lined paper and write a story about the picture. That day Sandy came home and joyfully announced, "Miss Ward had us write stories today!" From that moment school became fun so long as it included opportunities to write. Miss Ward saw possibilities in her young writer and encouraged her to keep writing.

This was especially a gift in light of the number of students Miss Ward was responsible to teach. In the school photo of Sandy's second-grade class there are forty-three (yes, *forty-three*) children. Miss Ward, in theory, should not have had time to give personal attention to any individual students, budding writers or otherwise; just teaching all those kids every day would have more than filled her time. And in that early wave of the Baby-Boomer generation—when there was no such thing as a teacher's aide—she probably had a similar number of students the year before that and the year after that. Yet Sandy cannot remember ever having a substitute teacher in elementary school.

At the time, Miss Ward's students thought she was something of a stern tyrant. Her discipline was strict and her expectations were high. She once leaned down and took an unruly boy by the shoulders and said "I like you! I like you to pieces! But I can't let you . . . [whatever it was he had done]." (Sandy remembers this because it was the first time she had ever heard the phrase "like you to pieces," and her writer's instincts took note of it!). She *had* to be that way, though; how else could one person stay in control of forty-three second-graders?

Every morning Miss Ward read to the class from the Bible. That wasn't unusual; all Sandy's teachers through fifth grade read from the Bible every morning. It wasn't until many years later that Sandy realized Miss Ward was a Christian teacher who fulfilled her calling because she loved God as well as her students. She stayed faithful to her calling for years. And more years. And decades. She always looked "old" but it was hard to pin down exactly how "old" she was.

Some forty years after high-school graduation and the gift of the teacup, we were living in Sandy's home town helping take care of her mother. Sandy took some Fiestaware and old cut glassware into a local antique shop to sell. The dealer said "I've got something here I think you'd like to have." He took a framed photograph off the wall and gave it to Sandy. It was a class picture of her mother's second-grade class (only twenty-one students). The teacher was Florence Ward! Somehow Sandy had forgotten or was never told that her second-grade teacher had also been her mother's second-grade teacher. And she had looked "old" even back then!

As a teacher Miss Ward was steadfast. She was faithful. Her Lord gave her the strength not merely to face forty-three children every day but to encourage, guide and discipline them with love.

From the example of Miss Ward's teaching career, we might conclude that all steadfastness is admirable, but steadfastness in and of itself is neither good nor bad. It depends on the direction in which a person is steadfast.

One time an older man told us he was distressed about his adult children because they were church-hopping. He believed they should remain faithful to their church and not shop around. "One of the most important things in life is consistency," he said, and went on to explain that if others see you being steadfast in your behavior, they'll know that you're dependable and that they can count on you.

Consistency in the wrong things, however, communicates a negative kind of dependability. Think of people who are consistently late or consistently dishonest or consistently lazy. They are "dependable" in the sense that we can depend on them to let us down and complicate our lives.

Christians who know God's faithfulness and who take his faithfulness as their pattern will be consistent in the right ways. Before the events in 2 Chronicles 20, Jehoshaphat appointed certain Levites, priests and heads of Israelite families to serve as administrators of God's law. Christians who live in the light of God's faithfulness—people like Miss Ward—will have the heart to follow Jehoshaphat's instructions to those administrators: "You must serve faithfully and wholeheartedly in the fear of the LORD" (2 Chronicles 19:9).

What's the main idea in this section?

What is one thing you can act on based on this reading?

PART 4. DISCUSS
Putting It All Together

OPEN

How do you feel when people are unfaithful to you?

READ 2 CHRONICLES 20:1-30.

Our society is becoming increasingly self-centered. People quickly discard spouses, friends and promises if they outlive their usefulness. Faithfulness applies to only one person—me. But when the Spirit develops this fruit in our lives, the results are quite different.

1. As a group, discuss your individual answers to question four from part one: How would Jehoshaphat's view of God encourage him and the people to trust God in this crisis?

2. From what you read in "Connect: Scripture to Scripture," how has God worked through faithful people to keep his promises?

3. How is Christ the ultimate expression of God's faithfulness?

4. "Reflect: A Faithful Teacher" mentioned two kinds of consistency. What makes the difference between them?

5. When the enemy army was advancing on Jerusalem, Jehoshaphat prayed to the Lord, "We do not know what to do, but our eyes are on you" (2 Chronicles 20:12). When have you prayed something similar?

6. What happened as a result of your prayer?

7. Hebrews 13:8 says, "Jesus Christ is the same yesterday and today and forever." Although Jesus does not change, as we mature spiritually our understanding of Jesus grows and goes through adjustments and corrections. What are some significant changes you have had in how you experience and think of Jesus?

8. Tell about a time or two when you have been most grateful for the fact that Jesus Christ does not change.

9. What relationship do you see between the faithfulness of God and keeping your promises?

10. All Christians are tempted to sin, but something that doesn't tempt one person at all may be a persistently tormenting temptation for another person. When do you (or when have you) most needed the faithfulness of God to overcome temptation (1 Corinthians 10:13)?

11. Who are some Christians you know who are especially faithful to their callings? If possible, make plans to talk with them about how the faithfulness of God encourages them and keeps them going.

12. Where do you especially need help following through on your commitments?

13. How can the members of your group help each other be faithful to your promises and commitments?

Thank God for his unending faithfulness to each of you and to those you care about. Pray especially about situations where you need to say, "We do not know what to do, but our eyes are on you" (2 Chronicles 20:12).

SESSION EIGHT

Gentleness

1 Thessalonians 2:1-12

WHERE WE'RE GOING

Part 1. Investigate: 1 Thessalonians 2:1-12 (On Your Own)

Part 2. Connect: Scripture to Scripture (On Your Own)

Part 3. Reflect: The Word of a Gentleman (On Your Own)

Part 4. Discuss: Putting It All Together (With a Group)

A PRAYER TO PRAY

Here's a prayer you can use to set you on your way:

Gentle Shepherd, we know you could push us around and force us to do what you want, but instead you lead us with tender prompting. If your full power were unleashed on us in all your righteousness, we would be undone. Instead, you are patient and tender-hearted toward us. Because you are gentle toward us, we can be gentle toward others. Yet we are so often harsh and demanding, unlike you. Help us treat others as you treat us, so that they will be gently drawn to you. We pray this in the name of the One who said "I am gentle and humble in heart." Amen.

PART 1. INVESTIGATE
1 Thessalonians 2:1-12

Read 1 Thessalonians 2:1-12.

2:7. *Well-to-do Romans often had slave or free wet nurses to care for young children, as did some, though fewer, lower-class Romans. According to the ideal of the educated Romans who could afford them, wet nurses should be educated so they could teach the young children; their most important trait, however, was their gentleness. They often endeared themselves to young children, who when they grew older frequently freed those nurses who had been slaves. The harshest Cynics criticized those who were gentle like wet nurses or the aged; others, like Dio Chrysostom (a public speaker who lived a generation after Paul), insisted that such gentleness should be cultivated.*

Many moralists, e.g., Plutarch, recommended that mothers nurse their own children rather than delegate the task to nursemaids, and this was no doubt the common practice for most people, who could not afford wet nurses anyway. The image could thus be one of a nursing mother, although all Paul's readers would have known of the custom of wet nurses as well.

1. According to Paul, what are some *wrong* ways to share Christ with others (vv. 3-6)?

2. Give an example of how we might make an appeal to a non-Christian using tricks or flattery.

3. In contrast, what were Paul's motives for sharing Christ with the Thessalonians?

   Why are pure motives so important?

4. How was Paul like a mother to the Thessalonians (vv. 7-9; some manuscripts have "were gentle" in verse 7)?

5. In what ways can we share "not only the gospel of God but our lives as well" with those around us?

What might this mean in terms of time, energy and vulnerability?

6. How was Paul also like a father to the Thessalonians (vv. 10-12)?

7. Why is it important for gentleness (v. 7) to be tempered with the qualities and goal mentioned in verse 12?

8. Looking back through the passage, how are the themes of evangelism and gentleness related?

2:9. *The Thessalonian Christians were poor (cf. 2 Cor 8:1-2) and did not share some of the Corinthians' objections to manual labor. The Christians in Philippi had sent him funds while he was in Thessalonica (Phil 4:15-16), but Paul still had to labor as an artisan. Because he could have set up shop in the marketplace, he could have done work and gained customers even if he was there only a brief time (Acts 17:2). Many Jewish teachers in this period had another trade besides teaching, often learned from their fathers.*

2:9. *"Night and day" was a common phrase, which could mean parts of the night and parts of the day. A manual laborer began work around sunrise and could talk with visitors while working; but from the early afternoon on Paul could use his time for more direct evangelism.*

2:10-11. *Although Romans valued the dignity of the stern father, most ancient portrayals of fathers (including Roman ones) stress their love, indulgence and concern for their children. True philosophers compared their concern for their hearers to that of a father as well as to that of a nurse (2:7), and disciples often saw teachers as paternal figures.*

2:12. *"Worthy" can mean appropriate to the dignity or standards of the person being honored; Jewish wisdom texts sometimes spoke of the righteous being "worthy of God." To new Christians who could no longer participate in the civic cult that honored the emperor in Thessalonica (1:9), God's "kingdom" may have had political overtones; recognizing their exclusive allegiance to God's kingdom would be costly.*

9. In what practical ways can we encourage, comfort and urge people to live lives worthy of God?

10. Think of those around you who require time, energy and vulnerability. How could you express your unique style of gentleness to those people?

Ask God to help you be an example of gentleness and sacrificial love to the people who came to mind for question ten.

THOUGHTS FROM HAZEL

The apostle Paul wrote these words to the church in Thessalonica: "As apostles of Christ we could have asserted our authority. Instead, we were like young children among you. Just as a nursing mother cares for her children, so we cared for you. Because we loved you so much, we were delighted to share with you not only the gospel of God but our lives as well." After reading this passage, I can almost see Paul gently stroking a fluffy white kitten—not what I usually think of when he comes to mind!

However, there is another side to gentleness, one my husband, Dave, calls "controlled strength." It comes out in a number of Paul's other letters (such as 1 Corinthians). I also see it often in Dave. I still remember one snowy Thanksgiving afternoon when our family was sitting in a circle around a roaring fire. I said, "It's a special day to be thankful. What if we go around the circle and say one thing we're thankful for in the person on our right?" Being used to this kind of thing from me, my family cooperated. Our oldest son, Larry, said of Dave, "I appreciate you for your controlled strength. Mom yaks a lot, but there's no one here that doubts you are the head of this house."

Oh, how true! And how much we Christians need to exercise this beautiful fruit of the Spirit—the "controlled strength" of gentleness.

PART 2. CONNECT
Scripture to Scripture

THE GENTLENESS OF GOD

God created everything. God holds the power of life and death over everything. God is sovereign over everything. Is it possible that a God with such ultimate power and authority could also be described as *gentle*?

While the word *gentle* does not often appear in the Bible as a characteristic of God, the *idea* of God's gentleness is all through Scripture. Even with that, though, it can be a difficult concept to pin down. Mary Evans comments, "Gentleness is a somewhat ambiguous concept in Hebrew and Greek as well as in English. The ambiguity arises from the fact that the term can denote both strength and vulnerability. . . . It is a characteristic of peaceable and controlled kindness, the opposite of arrogance or domination."[1]

A GENTLE EXODUS?

The story of the Israelites' getaway from Egypt hardly seems like a series of gentle events. Their deliverance from slavery was accompanied by ruinous plagues and the nationwide wailing of the Egyptians for dead firstborn sons. After escaping by night, the Israelites huddled at the edge of the Red Sea as Pharaoh's army approached. They saw the water open up for them to cross, and they saw the water close over their helpless pursuers. Their trek to the border of Canaan was a spiritual yo-yo of complaining, miracles, battles, worship and quarreling. When they got to Canaan, after all they had gone through to get there, they were afraid to enter the Promised Land and turned back.

Forty years later, when the new generation was about to enter Canaan at last, Moses recounted their journey. Read Deuteronomy 1:26-33.

Moses reminded the people, "You saw how the LORD your God carried you, as a father carries his son, all the way you went until you reached this place" (Deuteronomy 1:31). From what you know of the story of the exodus, what do you think Moses meant by "as a father carries his son"?

_____

_____

_____

_____

At the end of Deuteronomy, Moses recited the words of a song which again reiterated Israel's history up to that point. Read Deuteronomy 32:10-12. What was Israel's state "before" and "after" God chose them?

Before	After

HE TAUGHT THEM TO WALK

The prophet Hosea lived in the final days before Assyria conquered the northern kingdom of Israel in 722 B.C. His book of prophecy is known for its tender picture of God as the forgiving and redeeming husband of an unfaithful bride. Hosea also used imagery of a loving parent with a wayward child.

Read Hosea 11:1-11. Write out all the words and phrases which speak to you of God's gentleness:

_____

_____

_____

_____

_____

Paraphrase Hosea 11:3-4:

_____

_____

_____

_____

_____

RESCUED BY GOD

When the southern kingdom of Judah was conquered by Babylon and taken into exile for their idolatry, the Lord did not abandon them. He sent persistent messages to them through the prophet Ezekiel, who lived among the exiles. The Holy Spirit led Ezekiel to draw heart-wrenching word pictures about how God had dealt with and would deal with the Jewish people.

Read Ezekiel 16:1-14. Match up the Scripture passages with the events in Israel's history.

Israel is abandoned like an unwanted child.	verse 8
God passes by, takes notice and saves Israel's life.	verses 1-5
God pledges himself in a covenant with Israel.	verses 9-14
God cleanses Israel and adorns her with beauty.	verses 6-7

The word of the Lord through Ezekiel goes on to lament that Israel's dependence on God did not last. In sometimes repulsive detail, Ezekiel 16:15-58 relates the unfaithfulness of Israel. God hardly sounds gentle as he repeatedly calls Israel a prostitute. As a result of its idolatry, he explains, he will hand the nation over to those who will destroy her.

Then, when all sounds hopeless, comes the gentleness of the Lord. Read Ezekiel 16:59-63. (The "sisters" of v. 61 are Samaria and Sodom; see vv. 46-57.)

Mark the following statements as true or false.

_____ Israel would have to make atonement for her own sins.

_____ The covenant between God and Israel was destroyed because of Israel's idolatry.

_____ God himself would make atonement for Israel.

_____ Israel despised her covenant with God.

_____ God promised to establish a covenant which would never end.

_____ Israel will have a changed heart and new behavior.

Fill in the missing words in Ezekiel 16:60:

"Yet I will _____ the _____ I made with _____ in the days

of your youth, and I will establish an _____ covenant with you."

THE GENTLE KING COMES

God promised to "make atonement for you for all you have done" (Ezekiel 16:63). Yet even the prophet Ezekiel, who heard directly from the Lord, did not know when or how such atonement would be accomplished.

When King Cyrus and later King Darius of Persia allowed the Jews to return to their homeland from exile, one of the returnees was the prophet Zechariah. Although his book of prophecy includes calls to repentance, it is dominated by visions of abundant blessings, victory and peace.

Read Zechariah 9:9-17. In the latter part of this poem the Lord is portrayed as brandishing an arrow and a trumpet, but in the first part there is a different image. Write out the second half of verse 9, beginning with "See, your king comes to you."

_____

_____

_____

_____

It's impossible for Christians to read Zechariah 9:9 without thinking of Jesus' entry into Jerusalem, which we now commemorate yearly on Palm Sunday. Read Matthew 21:1-11 and John 12:12-19. Jesus' choice of a donkey on which to ride into Jerusalem "does not show him to be a poor or common man but a king, albeit one who does not conquer. Clearly he is innocent of the charge of rebelling against Caesar. A man on a donkey is not looking for war."[2]

Indeed, the gentleness of the king who rode into Jerusalem to die had been evident all through his earthly ministry.

Read Mark 10:13-16. Use your imagination to picture the scene in verse 16.

What do you see Jesus doing?

_____

_____

What expression do you see on his face?

_____

_____

_____

What expressions do you see on the faces of the children?

_____

_____

_____

What do you hear the children saying?

_____

_____

_____

What do you hear Jesus saying to them in return?

_____

_____

_____

Jesus' most overt declaration of his own gentleness is found Matthew 11:25-30. Fill in the missing parts of the passage:

"I praise you, Father, Lord of heaven and earth, because you have hidden these things from the wise and learned, and revealed them to _____. . . .

"Come to me, all you who are weary and burdened, and I will give you _____. Take my yoke upon you and learn from me, for _____, and you will find rest for your souls. For my yoke is _____."

---

[1]Mary J. Evans, "Gentleness," in *New Dictionary of Biblical Theology*, ed. T. Desmond Alexander and Brian S. Rosner (Downers Grove, IL: InterVarsity Press, 2000), p. 506.
[2]Leland Ryken, James C. Wilhoit and Tremper Longman III, gen. eds., "Donkey, Ass," in *Dictionary of Biblical Imagery* (Downers Grove, IL: InterVarsity Press, 1998), p. 215.

PART 3. REFLECT
The Word of a Gentleman

On a well-traveled road here in Rochester, Minnesota, there is a sign for "Gentling Dental Care." "Gentling" is the name of the dentist who started the business, but at first glance (and at forty miles per hour), the sign appears to say "Gentle Dental Care." And it grabs people's attention. Nobody wants to go to a dentist, but if you have to, who wouldn't hope for a *gentle* dentist?

As it turns out, a large number of dentists advertise with terms like *gentle dentist* or *gentle dentistry,* obviously attempting to reassure prospective patients. "Gentle dentistry" sounds like painless dentistry—where, we might imagine, all procedures are done in pillow-like chairs with bendable rubber instruments in pastel colors.

There is a limit, however, to just how *gentle* dentistry can be. Can a tooth be pulled gently? Can a cavity be drilled and filled gently? Can a root canal be done gently? Lidocaine might numb the mouth, but most dental procedures require some force.

Sandy remembers one particularly "forceful" dental procedure. Years ago she was running for exercise on an uneven street and stumbled. In a split-second decision, she scrambled to get her feet back under her and didn't put out her hands. As a result her unprotected face hit the asphalt. She managed to scoot herself to the side of the street but was alarmed to feel chips of broken teeth in her mouth. When she reached up and touched an upper front tooth, it came out in her hand—not broken off, but completely knocked out of her head (*avulsed,* she learned later).

Almost immediately a kind stranger pulled over and asked if Sandy needed help. "Yes" would have been an understatement! The driver took her home, and Dale rushed her—tooth in hand—to the dentist.

Because only a few minutes had passed since the accident, there was a chance the tooth could be saved. The dentist said he was going to try to reimplant it. Sandy doesn't remember feeling any pain, but she can testify that there is no *gentle* way to reimplant a knocked-out tooth. The dentist had to exert so much upward pressure that she felt like the tooth must surely be about to emerge from the top of her skull.

The dentist's strategy worked, though! The tooth "took" and enjoyed a ten-year second career before the root went bad. Afterward the dentist confessed it was the first reimplant he had ever done. Sandy was glad he didn't tell her that in advance. She also appreciated that the dentist kept asking her, "Are you doing okay?" and apologizing for the amount of force he had to use. While the tooth reimplantation required a lot of pressure, the dentist was being as gentle as possible under the circumstances.

In the case of Sandy's tooth, gentleness clearly did not equal weakness, but we often closely associate the two qualities. This is somewhat strange because the English word *gentle* does not have roots in any meaning of weakness. The word comes from the Latin *gens* which means "belonging to the same family" and has the same root as *genus* or *gene* or *generation.*

A *gentleman* or *gentlewoman* originally referred to a person born with high social status—the powerful people of a certain social rank. By that definition the summons at the start of the Indianapolis 500 is quite appropriate (whether or not it's altered for women drivers): "Gentlemen, start your engines!" Indy 500 drivers—men *and* women—are a powerful elite class unto themselves.

In time, *gentleman* or *gentlewoman* came to mean someone who exhibited a conscious and dignified restraint of power. In a democratic society, a *gentleman* (*gentlewoman* has fallen out of style) is one who acts with courtesy and refinement. He's not coarse or rude, but neither is he a wimp. He simply doesn't need to throw his weight around to prove his worth.

Our creator God has ultimate power, but he deals compassionately with his children. He does not have to impose his will on us in order to win our trust and love. In that sense, God is a *gentleman.*

Missionary David Livingstone experienced this aspect of God's character during a time of personal crisis. An Englishman of the nineteenth century who served in Africa, Livingstone faced imminent danger from the tribal people whom he wanted to reach with the gospel. He was tempted to run away under cover of night. In his journal he poured out his conflict about what to do. Jesus' words in Matthew 28:18-20 gave him strength. He wrote them in his journal in truncated form from the King James Version: "All power is given unto Me in heaven and in earth. Go ye therefore, and teach all nations, and lo, I am with you alway, even unto the end of the world."

Immediately afterward Livingstone wrote with confidence, "*It is the word of a gentleman of the most strict and sacred honour,* so there's an end of it! I will not cross furtively to-night as I intended. Should such a man as I flee? Nay, verily, I shall take observations for latitude and longitude to-night, though they may be the last. I feel quite calm now, thank God!"[1]

For David Livingstone, God was a *gentleman* whose word could be trusted. The concept is not so far from the scriptural idea of God's gentleness. The Creator of the universe is powerful, but he does not need to coerce with brute force. Because he is trustworthy, we can entrust our lives into his gentle hands.

One scholar has said, "Gentleness is an image of God's ultimate subversive power that undercuts the power structures of this world."[2] The gentleness of God is not weakness which caves in to opposition; it is strength which in time defeats the posturing and bullying of his enemies.

What's the main idea in this section?

What is one thing you can act on based on this reading?

---

[1] F. W. Boreham, "David Livingstone's Life Text," www.wholesomewords.org/missions/bliving8.html, italics added.
[2] Leland Ryken, James C. Wilhoit and Tremper Longman III, gen. eds., "Gentleness," in *Dictionary of Biblical Imagery* (Downers Grove, IL: InterVarsity Press, 1998), p. 325.

PART 4. DISCUSS
Putting It All Together

OPEN

Who is the most gentle person you know? Describe that person.

READ 1 THESSALONIANS 2:1-12.

The word *gentleness* conjures up wrong images for some people. It may denote a syrupy, self-denying quality or a quality which women have but "real men" do not. On the other hand, gentleness may be something we want very much, but we feel discouraged because the whole makeup of our personality is so far from being gentle. The apostle Paul's treatment of the Thessalonians provides a model of the gentleness God desires in us.

1. Look back at your individual answers to questions four and six in part one. As a group, discuss how Paul was like both a mother and a father to the Thessalonians.

2. What is significant about the fact that Paul and his associates did not wish to be a burden to the Thessalonians (v. 9)?

3. From what you learned in "Connect: Scripture to Scripture," how did the Lord show gentleness during Israel's escape from Egypt and trek toward the land of Canaan?

4. Because of their persistent idolatry, God allowed both the northern and southern kingdoms (Israel and Judah) to be conquered by pagan enemies. From what you saw in "Connect: Scripture to Scripture," what were some ways that God reassured his people that he was still concerned for them and had good plans for them?

5. How did Jesus display gentleness as great power under restraint?

6. The reading in part three quoted missionary David Livingstone as saying that God is a gentleman. In what senses would you agree or disagree, and why?

7. How have you experienced the gentleness of the Lord? Think of specific situations or insights.

8. Where or when are you tempted to *not* be gentle in the scriptural sense?

9. Where or when has the Holy Spirit prompted you to be gentle when you didn't want to be, and with what results?

10. Imagine a newcomer coming into your church fellowship for the first time. Do you think the visitor would have the impression that your church is a place of gentleness made up of gentle people? Explain why you answer as you do.

11. If you answered no to question ten, what could be done to make your church a gentler place in the biblical sense? Try to come up with more specific ideas than "Be nicer" or "Be more polite," although those may be a good start!

12. If you answered yes to question ten, what could be done to insure that visitors continue to experience gentleness when they come into your church, so the impression is not left to chance?

Think of people who could use gentleness from you. Pray that you will be filled with the Lord's gentleness toward those people. Ask the Lord to show you specific ways to minister to them this week.

SESSION NINE

Self-Control

1 Samuel 26

Where We're Going

Part 1. Investigate: 1 Samuel 26 (On Your Own)

Part 2. Connect: Scripture to Scripture (On Your Own)

Part 3. Reflect: Don't Eat That Marshmallow . . . Yet
(On Your Own)

Part 4. Discuss: Putting It All Together (With a Group)

A Prayer to Pray

Here's a prayer you can use to set you on your way:

Gracious God, we have been seeing how you perfectly manifest what Paul called the fruit of the Spirit. As we consider the final one, self-control, we do not want to imagine that you somehow struggle to master your own emotions. We are the ones who struggle with that. Fill us with such a clear purpose and vision for the life you have for us that we are not pulled away by lesser things. Keep us calm yet impassioned for service for you and others. We pray this in the name of the One who lived a life of perfect balance and freedom. Amen.

Part 1. Investigate
1 Samuel 26

Read 1 Samuel 26.

1. What do you learn about the character of each of the key people—David, Saul and Abishai—in this passage?

2. Put yourself in David's position (vv. 1-4). How might you feel toward someone who was trying in every way possible to kill you?

3. Describe the tension and dangers involved in David's plan (vv. 5-7).

4. Abishai tells David to seize this golden opportunity to kill Saul (v. 8). Why would this be a tempting suggestion?

5. Why does David resist the temptation to take matters into his own hands (vv. 9-11)?

6. When we are tempted to sin, how can our attitude toward God's will affect the outcome?

26:11. *The spear was generally used by the infantrymen in the front ranks. This is hardly where one would have expected to find a king. The fact that Saul always seems to have the spear near to hand (see for instance 1 Sam 18:10; 19:9; 2 Sam 1:6) suggests it may have been an insignia of his office. As a result, this may have been a ceremonial spear. It may also be significant that this is the same weapon he tried to kill David with in their early encounters. The jug or cruse may well have been one of the small disk-shaped vessels known from this period that featured two handles flanking the mouth so that they could be attached to a strap. Depriving a man of his water and weapon in this region would have constituted a threat to his life. David therefore demonstrated how Saul's life was in his hands.*

26:8-11. *David's refusal to kill Saul when he had the opportunity (see also 1 Samuel 24:1-22) is based on the king's status as the "Lord's anointed." He had been given his position by God and only God could* *take it from him. Political assassination is a very bad precedent for a claimant to a throne to employ (see the way in which it escalates in 1 Kings 15:25–16:27). Divine right to the throne could serve as an extraordinary insurance policy for the king as long as the mystique of being the "Lord's anointed" was maintained. Thus David's refusal to act demonstrates his loyalty to God's original designation of Saul as king and also provides an argument against future attempts on his own life when he became king. The person of the king was typically seen as being under the protection of deity in the ancient Near East. This is reflected, for instance, in a Hittite blessing on the king that affirms that the storm god will destroy anyone threatening the person of the king.*

26:20. *Hunting partridges involved beating the bushes and chasing the birds until they were exhausted. This is an apt description of the manner in which Saul has been pursuing David. There is also a pun here based on the literal meaning of the Hebrew word for partridge, which is the "one who calls upon the mountain" (see Jer 17:11). David is doing this as he reproaches King Saul.*

7. David and Abishai both attribute their actions to God. In the moment of temptation, how can we insure that we clearly discern God's will?

8. Notice how God helps David in verse 12. If we know God is present to help us in our struggle, how can it be easier to exercise self-control?

9. From a safe distance David calls out to Abner (vv. 13-16). How would his words to Abner make Saul more receptive to him?

10. What was Saul's response (vv. 17-25)?

11. What does this passage teach about how God regards human life (vv. 21-24)?

12. In what ways can our commitment to maintaining self-control so that we can do God's will affect Christians and non-Christians as they observe us?

Ask God's Spirit to cultivate the fruit of self-control within you.

THOUGHTS FROM HAZEL

In March of 2011, Dave's and my sixtieth wedding anniversary was approaching. My wedding gown lay in a box in our linen closet, carefully encased between sheets of tissue paper. The previous November, Dave and I had gotten it out, and with great fear and trembling, as well as considerable strength on Dave's part (it is a *heavy* satin gown!), I tried it on. Lo and behold, the zipper went up! We could hardly believe it. *Should we celebrate?* we wondered. *Do something really special? Renew our vows, and maybe rent a tux for Dave and do it in a church? Was it worth the effort?*

We called our family and got a resounding yes from them. Our neighbor, a PCA pastor, offered to officiate. The whole family would be able to come together from northern Ontario and Washington, D.C. Even our incredibly busy attorney-granddaughter in Toronto said she'd take time off to come and participate. It started to sound better and better.

There was one big hitch, though: Christmas was coming. And with it, the usual round of parties, big dinners, and gifts of nuts and candy (oh, how I love chocolate!). If that dress was still going to fit for our celebration, I couldn't gain a single pound!

I went to the Lord and drew on the fruit of self-control. With all the starving millions in the world, my prayer for self-control in my diet seemed about as important as a single grain of sand on a beach. But God gave me peace about sticking to my goal of not eating any sugar during the holidays.

The twenty-sixth of April came, and we celebrated in the beautiful church where we had been married back in 1951, with a dear friend singing the same songs we'd had in our wedding and all our grandchildren participating as the wedding party. Afterward we had a lavish reception, where our three sons told stories to our guests of how Jesus Christ had been magnified through us in their lives. It was a wonderful day! And my dress fit perfectly.

In the grand scheme of life, sticking to my "no sugar" rule over Christmas and having my wedding dress still fit me in April was surely a little thing. And yet it was big, too, because I couldn't have done it alone. It happened only as I drew on the fruit of self-control and trusted the Spirit who gives it.

PART 2. CONNECT
Scripture to Scripture

TWO GOLDEN OPPORTUNITIES

David knew that God had chosen him to replace Saul as king of Israel. He remembered the time, years back, when he was called in from tending his father's sheep, and the prophet Samuel anointed him from a horn of oil, which was the sign of God's special choosing. The Spirit of the Lord came on David from that day on (1 Samuel 16:12-13).

Years earlier Samuel had anointed Saul as king (1 Samuel 10:1). David knew Saul very well, having served as his harpist, armor-bearer, military captain and son-in-law. And he knew that Saul was desperate to keep his power; he was not about to abdicate the throne to David. In fact, Saul was set on getting rid of David altogether.

David spent years on the run from Saul, building up his own following and military reputation. During that time he had two golden opportunities to kill Saul. One was in a cave where Saul was in an embarrassingly vulnerable position (1 Samuel 24) and the other was the situation we studied in part one (1 Samuel 26), when Saul's supposed guardians left him unprotected.

Read 1 Samuel 24:1-7 and compare it with 1 Samuel 26:5-11. David clearly had a problem—King Saul. Here were two perfect opportunities to take care of the problem. However, David also wanted to be loyal to the Lord, who had chosen Saul to be king. He had to act in one way or the other. David chose to restrain himself. His golden opportunities to kill Saul turned into golden opportunities to exhibit self-control.

Respond to the following questions by writing "yes" or "no" in the blanks. Then write the verse numbers that led you to your conclusion.

In both instances, did other people urge David to kill Saul because it looked like God had arranged circumstances to make it possible? _____

Verse(s):

Did David refer to Saul as "the Lord's anointed" in only one of the instances? _____

Verse(s):

Did David believe that God himself would strike Saul at the right time? _____

Verse(s):

Did David display boldness in one case and timidity in the other? _____

Verse(s):

Did David risk the disapproval of his fighting companions when he restrained himself? _____

Verse(s):

SELF-CONTROL FAILURE

After he became king of Israel, David did not always exhibit the self-control he showed during his years on the run. Read 2 Samuel 11:1—12:25. At each point in the account, identify what David *did* and what he *could have done* (that which would have been a self-controlled response).

	What David Did (lack of self-control)	**What David Could Have Done** (showing self-control)
2 Samuel 11:1-5		
2 Samuel 11:6-13		
2 Samuel 11:14-26		

In 2 Samuel 11:6-13, how did Uriah the Hittite—the wronged husband—demonstrate the self-control that David lacked?

_____

_____

_____

_____

_____

_____

DOES GOD SHOW SELF-CONTROL?

We could cite many people throughout the Bible who either did or did not show self-control, or, like David, showed both at different times. Throughout this study guide, however, we have tried to look at how the fruits of the Spirit reflect the character of God. The other fruits have been easy to see: love, joy, peace, patience, kindness, goodness, faithfulness and gentleness. Now what about self-control? Where do we see God exhibiting this fruit?

If we take *self-control* to mean "restraint," we can find plenty of places in Scripture where God restrained his righteous anger. Scripture reiterates that the Lord is *slow to anger* (see, for example, Exodus 34:6; Numbers 14:18; Nehemiah 9:17; Joel 2:13).

For one of the most noteworthy instances of God restraining his anger, read Exodus 32:1-14. Moses was on Mt. Sinai receiving the Ten Commandments. Meanwhile the people waiting at the foot of the mountain grew impatient.

God reacted to the Israelites' idolatry by threatening to _____.

Moses argued that if God destroyed the Israelites, the Egyptians would _____.

Moses reminded God about _____.

In response to Moses' words, God _____.

Consider again where the Israelites were and how recently they had been miraculously delivered from Egypt. Why was their idolatry at that time and place an especially shocking affront to the Lord?

_____

_____

_____

_____

_____

Why would God have been justified in destroying all the idolaters?

_____

_____

_____

_____

_____

I KNEW IT!

For another instance of God restraining his anger, read the book of Jonah.

Paraphrase how God responds to Nineveh's repentance (Jonah 3:10):

_____

_____

_____

_____

_____

We don't find out why Jonah fled from God's call until the last chapter of the book. Paraphrase Jonah's complaint (Jonah 4:1-3):

_____

_____

_____

_____

_____

_____

Mark the following statements as true or false:

_____ The Lord restrained his anger because Jonah prayed.

_____ Jonah showed less self-control than God showed.

_____ The Lord would have had every right to destroy Nineveh.

_____ Jonah had every right to feel angry.

_____ The Lord showed restraint toward Jonah as well as toward Nineveh.

PITY AND WRATH

We can find many other instances in the Bible where God restrained his righteous anger. He could have wiped out individual people and didn't. He could have wiped out nations and didn't. In human terms we could say that God showed self-control.

But does God *always* show self-control? For all the times Scripture reveals him holding himself back, there are plenty of other passages where he seems to lash out in uncontrolled fury.

Read 2 Chronicles 36:11-20. Verses 15-16 are a "hinge" in the passage—the point where God's self-control appears to run out and he unleashes his anger. Fill in the key words for these two verses:

The LORD, the God of their fathers, sent _____ to them through his messengers _____ and _____, because he had _____ on his people and on his dwelling place. But they _____ God's messengers, _____ his words and _____ at his prophets until the _____ of the LORD was aroused against his people and there was no remedy.

What's going on here? Did God just lose his temper? Blow his stack? Fly off the handle?

The passage says that the *wrath* of the Lord was aroused. How does verse 14 encapsulate the reason for God's wrath?

_____

_____

_____

_____

God had laid out a fundamental rule for his people. Jesus would later call it the first and greatest commandment. "Hear, O Israel: The LORD our God, the LORD is one. Love the LORD your God with all your heart and with all your soul and with all your strength" (Deuteronomy 6:4-5). It is God's desire that people put him first, but his command is not arbitrary or egotistical. It is for our own good, because he loves us.

When God allowed the floodgates to open and the Babylonians to conquer the Israelites, it might seem to us that he had thrown off all restraint and self-control, but his intention—which he had tried over and over to communicate to them in less painful ways—was ultimately to turn the people from their idolatry and bring them back to himself. The wrath of God is not inconsistent with the love of God. Both the mercy of God and the wrath of God show the consistency of his purposes.

We are made to love and worship God; this is what he consistently wants us to do. His commitment to our good does not fluctuate with his moods. He does not capriciously give in to the temptation to lose his temper at us. He has a consistent commitment to our holiness, and he has a consistent hatred of sin. His actions always spring from his perfect wisdom and deep love for us, and are intended for our ultimate good—to make us more holy, more like himself.

AWAY FROM ME, SATAN!

God's self-control is seen clearly in the New Testament through Jesus Christ, God incarnate, as Jesus was a man of perfect self-control. Immediately after his baptism, the Holy Spirit led him into the desert, where he was tempted by Satan. Read Matthew 4:1-11. Fill in this chart for the three temptations:

The Temptation	What Jesus Could Have Done	What He Did Instead

STRANGE INSTRUCTIONS

Jesus' pattern of self-control continued all through his earthly life. What was the temptation for Jesus in each of the following passages from the Gospel of Mark?

Mark 1:32-34

Mark 3:11-12

Mark 5:41-43

Mark 7:33-36

Mark 9:2-9

Why do you think Jesus gave the instructions he did?

_____

_____

_____

_____

_____

Read John 6:14-15. The "sign" that Jesus had performed was the miraculous feeding of five thousand men (plus women and children) with five loaves of bread and two fish. After that miracle, his popularity soared! People began to say, "Surely this is the Prophet who is to come into the world," which of course is exactly who Jesus was. It seems like it would have been the perfect time for him to take advantage of this surge in his popularity.

Under such adrenaline-raising circumstances, how did Jesus show remarkable self-control?

_____

_____

_____

_____

_____

TAKING CHARGE

Jesus did not always manifest his self-control by withdrawing and staying quiet. Read Mark 11:15-18. What indications do you see that Jesus' actions in the temple were not just a fit of uncontrolled temper?

_____

_____

_____

_____

_____

THE WAY OUT—NOT TAKEN

Nowhere did Jesus display greater self-control than during his final hours. His calm restraint in the face of ferocious brutality is sometimes almost too painful to read, but we must read it to appreciate how deeply self-control was ingrained in his character.

Read Matthew 26:47-56. Write out verse 53 word for word.

_____

_____

_____

_____

At this time in Roman history, a *legion* was six thousand soldiers.[1] *Twelve legions of angels* would therefore have been seventy-two thousand angels, and Jesus could have asked his Father for even more! Try to imagine seventy-two thousand–plus angels angels arriving in Gethsemane that night. What would that have looked like? What would it have sounded like? What would have been the results? Describe what you imagine.

_____

_____

_____

_____

What reason did Jesus give for exercising restraint and *not* asking his Father for those angels?

_____

_____

_____

_____

Throughout his whole trial and crucifixion, Jesus showed utmost self-possession and courage. Here was God incarnate willingly putting himself into the cruel hands of sinful people. He could have crushed them all into nothingness, but he restrained himself.

Read Matthew 27:32-44. Jesus was mocked for his apparent powerlessness. What did people challenge him to do?

_____

_____

_____

_____

Why do you think Jesus did *not* do as they insisted?

_____

_____

_____

_____

In the life of Jesus Christ we see the self-control that God has always shown in the face of human sin—a self-control that knows when grace is needed and when truth and even confrontation are needed. He is never indecisive or weak, never thoughtless or careless with his actions. Rather, in his loving wisdom he knows when to hold back and when to act—all for our good.

---

[1]John H. Walton, Victor H. Matthews and Mark W. Chavalas, *The IVP Bible Background Commentary: Old Testament* (Downers Grove, IL: InterVarsity Press, 2000), p. 122.

PART 3. REFLECT
Don't Eat That Marshmallow . . . Yet

Distracted by email and social media? If you're a Mac user, you can get help. An application called SelfControl will, at least in theory, keep you focused on your work. It locks out those distractions so you can't get at them no matter how much you try.

The website for SelfControl describes it this way: "SelfControl is an OS X application which blocks access to incoming and/or outgoing mail servers and websites for a predetermined period of time. For example, you could block access to your email, Facebook, and Twitter for 90 minutes, but still have access to the rest of the web. Once started, it can not be undone by the application or by restarting the computer, you must wait for the timer to run out."[1]

Despite its optimistic name, the SelfControl does not, ironically, develop *self*-control at all. In place of inner strength of character, it supplies only an electronic padlock. It offers artificial restraint from the outside rather than restraint of the self from within. The frustrated Mac user, denied access to email, can still grab a hammer and smash something (perhaps the very Mac which contains SelfControl?).

If we adults struggle with self-control, how much self-control can we expect of a four-year-old child? In the late 1960s, researchers carried out psychological experiments at Bing Nursery School on the campus of Stanford University. The procedure was uncomplicated: A child was led into a room containing a desk and chair. On the desk were several kinds of treats. The child could select a favorite—for example, a marshmallow.

The researcher then left each child alone with one marshmallow and a choice. They could eat the one marshmallow right away and ring a bell to signal the researcher, or they could wait until the researcher returned and get *two* marshmallows. Hidden cameras recorded the children's reactions as they fought their inner marshmallow wars. Most of them gave in and gobbled the treat, but about 30 percent waited until the researcher came back.

At the time, psychologists assumed that children's ability to wait depended on how badly they wanted the marshmallow. But it soon became obvious that *every* child craved the extra treat. What, then, determined self-control? Psychologist Walter Mischel's conclusion, based on hundreds of hours of observation, was that the crucial skill was the "strategic allocation of attention." Instead of getting obsessed with the marshmallow—the "hot stimulus"—the patient children distracted themselves by covering their eyes, pretending to play hide-and-seek underneath the desk, or singing songs from *Sesame Street*. Their desire wasn't defeated—it was merely forgotten. "If you're thinking about the marshmallow and how delicious it is, then you're going to eat it," Mischel says. "The key is to avoid thinking about it in the first place."

After publishing some papers on his research, Mischel moved on to other projects. In later years he began to hear from his own children (fellow students of the research subjects) that the children who had waited for their treat were having better academic success than those who had eaten their treat immediately. He became curious enough to follow up.

Mischel sent out a questionnaire to all the reachable parents, teachers, and academic advisers of the six hundred and fifty-three subjects who had participated in the marshmallow task, who were by then in high school. He asked about every trait he could think of, from their capacity to plan and think ahead to their ability to "cope well with problems" and get along with their peers. He also requested their S.A.T. scores.

Mischel analyzed the results and discovered that the children who had eaten the first marshmallow right away struggled more with behavioral problems, both at home and at school, as they grew up. Their S.A.T. scores were lower. They had trouble handling stress, paying attention and maintaining friendships. By contrast, the children who had waited had S.A.T. scores averaging 210 points higher than the impatient children.

Today Mischel emphasizes the mental and emotional importance of forming the habit of delaying gratification—waiting, so to speak, for the second marshmallow.

According to Mischel, even the most mundane routines of childhood—such as not snacking before dinner, or saving up your allowance, or holding out until Christmas morning—are really sly exercises in cognitive training: we're teaching ourselves how to think so that we can outsmart our desires. But Mischel isn't satisfied with such an informal approach. "We should give marshmallows to every kindergartner," he says. "We

should say, 'You see this marshmallow? You don't have to eat it. You can wait. Here's how.'"[2]

Young children can begin to learn self-control and will benefit from forming the habit of controlling their impulses. Some will be better at it than others.

The good news of the gospel is that it's not too late for any of us. With Christ living within, even the most recklessly impulsive and self-indulgent adult can change and begin to manifest self-control. Genuine self-control is a spiritual matter. The Bible calls it a fruit of the Holy Spirit.

A Christian in tune with the Spirit sees self-control as freedom—both freedom to choose a better way and freedom from sin's control. We do not *have* to indulge all those petty sinful thoughts and actions that pester us daily. We do not *have* to join in when people criticize a fellow believer; neither do we *have* to congratulate ourselves for keeping quiet. The Holy Spirit has a better way for us. We are not Jesus Christ and will never have his masterful self-control, but his Spirit within us will lovingly manage our impulses if we allow *him* to control us.

What's the main idea in this section?

What is one thing you can act on based on this reading?

[1]See www.macupdate.com/app/mac/31289/selfcontrol (accessed March 8, 2012).
[2]Jonah Lehrer, "Don't! The Secret of Self-Control," *The New Yorker*, May 18, 2009, www.newyorker.com/reporting /2009/05/18/090518fa_fact_lehrer?currentPage=all (accessed March 8, 2012).

PART 4. DISCUSS
Putting It All Together

OPEN
In what area of your life would you like to have greater self-control?

READ 1 SAMUEL 26.
Saul was anointed king over Israel. But because he was disobedient, God took the kingdom from him and gave it to David. As a result, Saul's wrath and jealousy were kindled toward David, and he tried to kill him at every opportunity. In 1 Samuel 26 David faces the powerful temptation of choosing self-gratification over self-control. His response can encourage us in our struggles.

1. Why does David resist the temptation to take matters into his own hands (vv. 9-11)? (You may want to look back at your individual answers for question five from part one to aid in your discussion.)

2. People often think of God as vengeful and angry, especially in the Old Testament. From what you learned in the "Connect: Scripture to Scripture" section, how has God displayed self-control through the ages?

3. What is the connection between the purposes of God for humanity and God's self-control?

4. Identify some examples of the self-control of Jesus Christ which especially stand out for you.

5. In the "marshmallow experiment" described in part three, the children who succeeded in waiting managed to distract themselves from the treat. What biblical strategies can Christians use to maintain self-control?

6. When have you experienced the Holy Spirit helping you be more self-controlled?

7. In what areas of your life do you tend to be too impulsive and need to restrain yourself?

8. In what areas of your life do you tend to be too passive and need self-control to be bolder?

9. What relationship do you see between self-control and courage?

10. Who has helped you to be more self-controlled, and how did this person help you?

11. In times of temptation, how do you usually pray?

Pray for each other—that the Holy Spirit will work genuine self-control in each of you, in both thoughts and actions.

Guidelines for Leaders

My grace is sufficient for you.

2 Corinthians 12:9

*I*f leading a small group is something new for you, don't worry. You don't need to be an expert on the Bible or a trained teacher. The discussion guides in part four are designed to facilitate a group's discussion, not a leader's presentation. Guiding group members to discover together what the Bible has to say and to listen together for God's guidance will help them remember much more than a lecture would. Furthermore, the discussion guides are designed to flow naturally. You may even find that the discussions seem to lead themselves! They're also flexible; you can use the discussion guide with a variety of groups—students, professionals, coworkers, friends, neighborhood or church groups. Each discussion takes forty-five to sixty minutes in a group setting.

There are some important facts to know about group dynamics and helpful discussion. The suggestions listed below should equip you to effectively and enjoyably fulfill your role as leader.

Preparing for the Study

1. Ask God to help you understand and apply the passage in your own life. Unless this happens, you will not be prepared to lead others. Pray too for the various members of the group. Ask God to open your hearts to the message of his Word and motivate you to action.

2. Carefully work through parts one, two and three of each session before your group meets. Spend time in meditation and reflection as you consider how to respond.

3. Write your thoughts and responses in the space provided in the study guide. This will help you to express your understanding of the passage clearly and more easily remember significant ideas you want to highlight in the group discussion.

4. It may help to have a Bible dictionary handy. Use it to look up any unfamiliar words, names or places.

5. Reflect seriously on how you need to apply the Scripture to your life. Remember that the group members will follow your lead in responding to the studies. They will not go any deeper than you do.

Leading the Study

1. At the beginning of your first time together, explain that these studies are meant to be discussions, not lectures. Encourage the members of the group to participate. However, do not put pressure on those who may be hesitant to speak—especially during the first few sessions.

2. Be sure that everyone in your group has a study guide. Encourage the group to prepare beforehand for each discussion by reading the introduction to the guide and by working through the questions in each study.

3. Begin each study on time. Open with prayer, asking God to help the group understand and apply the passage.

4. Discuss the "Open" question before the Bible passage is read. It introduces the

theme of the study and helps group members begin to open up. It can also reveal where our thoughts and feelings need to be transformed by Scripture. Encourage as many members as possible to respond to the "Open" question, and be ready to get the discussion going with your own response.

5. Have a group member read aloud the passage to be studied as indicated in the guide.

6. The study questions are designed to be read aloud just as they are written. You may, however, prefer to express them in your own words.

   Note also that there may be times when it is appropriate to deviate from the discussion guide. For example, a question may have already been answered. If so, move on to the next question. Or someone may raise an important question not covered in the guide. Take time to discuss it, but try to keep the group from going off on tangents.

7. Avoid answering your own questions. An eager group quickly becomes passive and silent if members think the leader will do most of the talking. If necessary, repeat or rephrase the question until it is clearly understood, or refer to the commentary woven into the guide to clarify the context or meaning.

8. Don't be afraid of silence in response to the discussion questions. People may need time to think about the question before formulating their answers.

9. Don't be content with just one answer. Ask, "What do the rest of you think?" or "Anything else?" until several people have given answers to the question.

10. Try to be affirming whenever possible. Especially affirm participation. Never reject an answer; if it is clearly off-base, ask, "Which verse led you to that conclusion?" or again, "What do the rest of you think?"

11. Don't expect every answer to be addressed to you, even though this will probably happen at first. As group members become more at ease, they will begin to truly interact with each other. This is one sign of healthy discussion.

12. Don't be afraid of controversy. It can be very stimulating. If you don't resolve an issue completely, don't be frustrated. Explain that the group will move on and God may enlighten all of you in later sessions.

13. Periodically summarize what the group has said about the passage. This helps to draw together the various ideas mentioned and gives continuity to the study. But don't preach.

14. Conclude your time together with the prayer suggestion at the end of the study, adapting it to your group's particular needs as appropriate. Ask for God's help in following through on the applications you've identified.

15. End on time.

Many more suggestions and helps for studying a passage or guiding discussion can be found in *How to Lead a LifeGuide Bible Study* and *The Big Book on Small Groups* (both from InterVarsity Press/USA).

BIBLIOGRAPHY

Alexander, T. Desmond, and Brian S. Rosner, eds. *New Dictionary of Biblical Theology*. Downers Grove, IL: InterVarsity Press, 2000.

Alexander, T. Desmond, and David W. Baker, eds. *Dictionary of the Old Testament: Pentateuch*. Downers Grove, IL: InterVarsity Press, 2003.

Beale, G. K., and D. A. Carson. *Commentary on the Old Testament Use of the New Testament*. Grand Rapids: Baker Academic, 2007.

Brown, Raymond. *The Message of Numbers*. The Bible Speaks Today. Downers Grove, IL: InterVarsity Press, 2002.

Buttrick, George Arthur. *Interpreter's Dictionary of the Bible*. Vol. 1. Nashville: Abingdon Press, 1962.

Harris, R. Laird, and Ronald Youngblood. Note on Lev 3:1. In *The NIV Study Bible*, edited by Kenneth Barker et al. Grand Rapids: Zondervan, 1995.

Keller, Timothy. *The Reason for God: Belief in an Age of Skepticism*. New York: Riverhead Books, 2008.

Lamb, David. *God Behaving Badly: Is the God of the Old Testament Angry, Sexist and Racist?* Downers Grove, IL: InterVarsity Press, 2011.

Larsen, Dale, and Sandy Larsen. *Living Your Legacy: An Action-Packed Guide for the Later Years*. Downers Grove, IL: InterVarsity Press, 2012.

Marshall, I. Howard, A. R. Millard, J. I. Packer and D. J. Wiseman, eds. *New Bible Dictionary*. 3rd ed. Downers Grove, IL: InterVarsity Press, 1996.

Motyer, J. Alec. *Isaiah*. Tyndale Old Testament Commentaries. Downers Grove, IL: InterVarsity Press, 1999.

Packer, J. I. *Knowing God*. Downers Grove, IL: InterVarsity Press, 1993.

Ryken, Leland, James C. Wilhoit and Tremper Longman III, gen. eds. *Dictionary of Biblical Imagery*. Downers Grove, IL: InterVarsity Press, 1998.

Vine, W. E., Merrill F. Unger and William White Jr. *Vine's Complete Expository Dictionary of Old and New Testament Words*. Nashville: Thomas Nelson, 1996.

Walton, John H., Victor H. Matthews and Mark W. Chavalas. *The IVP Bible Background Commentary: Old Testament*. Downers Grove, IL: InterVarsity Press, 2000.

Wenham, G. J., J. A. Motyer, D. A. Carson and R. T. France, eds. *New Bible Commentary*. 21st century ed. Downers Grove, IL: InterVarsity Press, 1994.

Wilson, William. *Wilson's Old Testament Word Studies*. Peabody, MA: Hendrickson, 1900.

Witherington, Ben, III. "From Hesed to Agape: What's Love Got to Do with It?" *Bible Review*, December 2003. Accessed December 6, 2011. www.basarchive.org/sample/bswbBrowse.asp?PublD=BSBR&Volume=19&Issue=6&ArticleID=7.